SUCCESSFUL Infant Feeding

SUCCESSFUL
Infant Feeding

Ensuring your baby thrives on the
BREAST or **BOTTLE**

HEATHER WELFORD

Carroll & Brown Publishers Limited

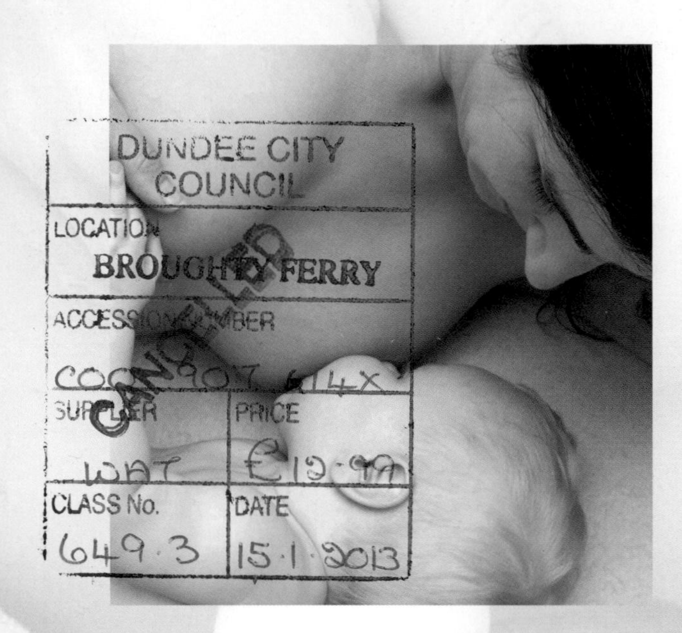

First published in 2011 in the United Kingdom by

Carroll & Brown Publishers Limited
20 Lonsdale Road
London NW6 6RD

Managing Art Editor Emily Cook
Photography Jules Selmes

A CIP catalogue record for this book is available
from the British Library.

ISBN 978 1 907952 01 2

10987654321

Reproduced by RALI, Spain
Printed and bound in China

Contents

Introduction

This book is about feeding your baby – but while it includes a great deal of 'how to do it' and information related to the health, comfort and wellbeing of both of you, its aim is to do rather more than that.

I have worked as a breastfeeding supporter and a trainer of other breastfeeding supporters for many years, with the UK's major parenting charity. Over time, I've come to see how important feeding is to the way mothers feel about themselves, and how important it is to their growing relationship with their babies. It's always been clear to me that there's more to 'feeding babies' than a physical behaviour, much more than a transfer of nutrients from a mother to her child. It's a complex interaction, rich in cultural, social and emotional aspects and the usual question 'breast or bottle?' does not reflect much of this.

Breast milk or formula milk is sometimes presented as a straight choice, as if it was simply a matter of personal preference. Health promotion with mothers is aimed at increasing the numbers who breastfeed with a sort of 'information in equals behaviour out' equation as if all that's needed is to tell you breastfeeding is important for your baby's health, and you will overcome any of the barriers to it as a result.

In fact, in most of the developed world, mothers are not 'breastfeeding mothers' or 'formula-feeding mothers'. Most – virtually all, in fact – are both. The majority of mothers (76 per cent in the UK) begin breastfeeding, but almost half of them start to use formula alongside breastfeeding by the time their baby is a week old; by six weeks, about half of all babies are fully formula fed. But nine out of 10 of the mothers who stop breastfeeding by six weeks say they would have liked to

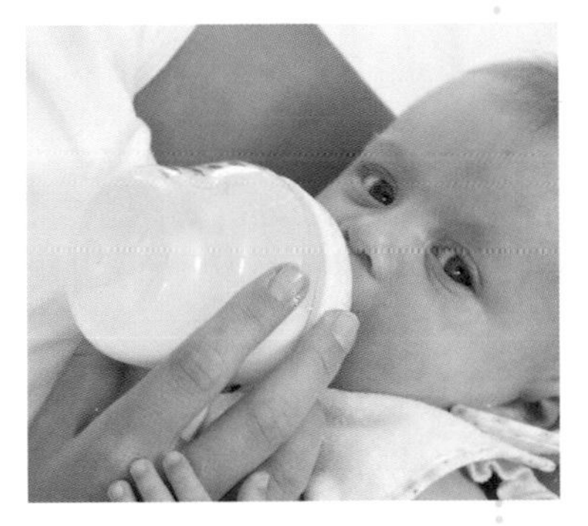

continue. I think this is saddening, but what I don't want to see are formula-feeding mothers believing that they and their babies are being judged. There are many ways breastfeeding can be encouraged and supported without criticising individuals who may have their own reasons for using formula, in place of or alongside breastfeeding and it's no one's job to decide if the reasons are 'good' ones or not.

It's certainly the case, however, that given the right circumstances, more women would be able to breastfeed for longer and this would have important and measurable public health benefits, for sure. But there are also important and probably not quite so measurable emotional and psychological benefits for mothers who manage to achieve what they planned to do, and enjoy it, too, so it would be desirable if the barriers to breastfeeding could be overcome by better support and information and through public acceptance of breastfeeding.

In the future, I would like to see fewer babies being formula fed – but in the meantime, I hope to help these mothers and babies feed happily and comfortably, and in a way that enhances their loving, close relationship with each other. If you use formula, there's no reason not to have this, too.

Feeding your baby – however it's done – is more than just a way of making sure he or she gets sufficient food to grow. It's more than just satisfying your baby's hunger and thirst. It's a major part of your relationship with your baby, and it should be rewarding, comfortable, pleasurable, unstressed and rich in communication and social connection for both of you.

This book will tell you how this can be done.

Heather Welford

CHAPTER 1

Your baby's needs in the first year

Your baby came into the world totally dependent on your intensive, responsive care for his survival. Unlike many animals – who manage to get to their feet minutes after birth, and can move purposefully and without help – human babies take a long time to manage anything close to independence.

Although your baby was born capable of a great deal and primed to learn a lot more, at birth he is still essentially under-equipped, with a massive amount of growth still to take place, and with his brain development some years away from maturity.

In his first 12 months, your baby needs sustenance to survive and grow, as well as to ensure his intellectual, emotional, social and psychological development. Such sustenance comes entirely from his environment – and his environment is you.

Nutritional needs

Breast milk: the perfect food for life and growth

Fossil evidence and evolutionary science indicate that the first mammals – animals whose females give birth to live young and produce milk for them – appeared some 200 million years ago and, as each species evolved, the milk it made eventually became species specific. The species Homo, from which humans evolved, appeared about 2.5 million years ago, while beings physiologically identical to us appeared approximately 200,000 years ago. Getting the 'right' milk for human babies took some time, and just as the female elephant, giraffe, gorilla, dog, sheep and cat, and so on, produce milk whose contents and mode of delivery match the precise needs of their young, so human milk evolved to deliver what human babies need.

One example of this perfect match is the iron content of human milk, which is low compared with cows' milk. A human baby has his own iron stores, built up during his mother's pregnancy, so his need for iron in breast milk is less than a calf's. The iron which is there, however, is uniquely bio-available – that is, it is easily processed and used by the baby. This is because breast milk has comparatively high levels of vitamin C and lactose, and other constituents, which aid the absorption of iron.

In addition, human milk protein is made up predominantly of whey proteins, which form soft and fluffy curds in the stomach. This texture promotes quick and easy digestion. Cows' milk, on the other hand, is made up predominantly of casein proteins, which form tougher, less digestible curds. Quick digestion is allied with frequent feeding, which is ideally suited to the small size of a human infant's stomach and his need for constant loving contact – both of which are important for him to thrive physically and emotionally. Most infant formulas are based on cows' milk, but some types undergo processing so that whey proteins predominate and iron content is reduced (see pages 40–1).

In order to meet your baby's nutritional needs, your breast milk changes in quality and quantity as he grows. A newborn baby, for example, needs to expel the contents of his bowel, and colostrum – the first milk – has a laxative effect that helps him do so. He also needs to be protected from any pathogens that may be present in his new environment and colostrum is high in antibody-rich proteins. From about three or four days after the birth, your mature breast milk with its energy-boosting fats becomes available, and your baby is able to take in larger volumes, growing as a result. A newborn's initial weight loss due to bowel emptying will be replaced by weight gain. To a large extent, your baby ensures he stimulates the 'right' quantity of breast milk: he removes what he needs and if you keep him close and respond to his needs promptly and reliably you'll make enough milk for him. It's only when there are particular challenges – if your baby is born pre-term, becomes ill or is unable to feed effectively or often enough for some reason – that you might need to take the initiative and deliberately feed him more often to increase your milk production (see pages 82–3).

UNDERSTANDING GUIDELINES

You might read or be told about guidelines on infant feeding, issued as an official recommendation designed to promote good health. Issued by the World Health Organisation, official guidelines state that six months' exclusive breastfeeding, followed by continued breastfeeding alongside other foods, gives babies the healthiest start to life. It doesn't mean that all babies need something more than breast milk at exactly the same age – six months – and that anything sooner or later than this is somehow harmful. In reality, that exact date is what comes out of research, which used six months as a convenient line. All babies are different but most healthy ones reach the stage of happily moving on to include other foods in their diet at some time around the middle of their first year. For more on the whole subject of introducing solids, a development stage known as weaning, see pages 122–5.

BUILDING THE BRAIN

Humans are born immature, and as a result we are highly dependent on carers for everything we need to survive for a long time.

Evolutionary anthropology – the study of how we became human – says that the reason for our relative lack of 'completion' at birth is the fact that we walk on two legs. This freed up our hands to make tools, which improved survival skills, and ultimately led to the development of a bigger brain and higher intelligence.

The female pelvis and birth canal narrowed because of our upright posture and, as a result, there was less room to carry an infant for longer. This means birth has to take place before the baby's brain reaches its full size; at the time of birth, the infant brain is just 25 per cent of its final size. This is not actually a disadvantage. The fact that an infant's brain is still under construction at birth makes perfect social sense – with plenty of growing still to do, a baby's brain is able to adapt to the community to which he belongs.

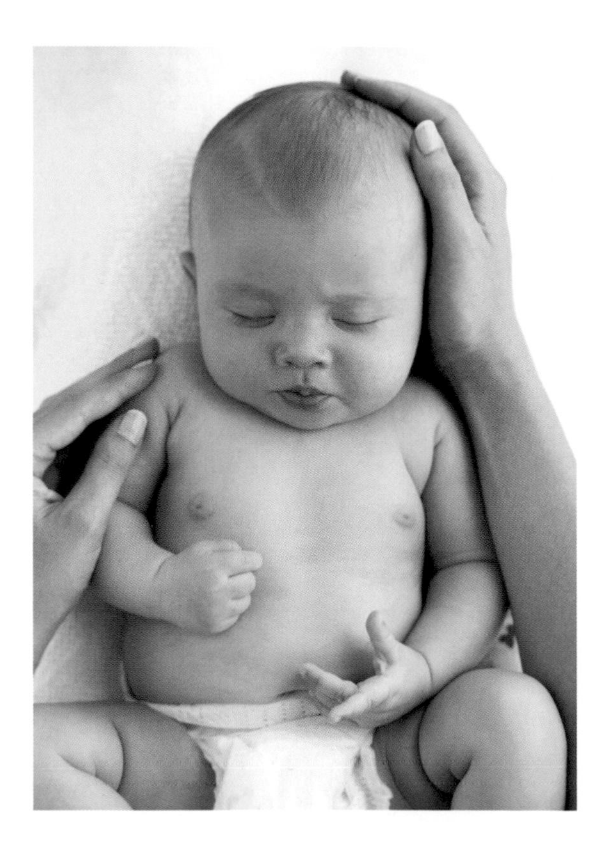

The brain which matures from the one we're born with allows us (or in this case, our babies) to become thinking, judging, loving, learning beings; it enables us to remember and enjoy, or to feel sad or happy. Eventually, it allows us to imagine what it might feel like to be someone else, which is the root of empathy and moral (or amoral) behaviour. While the brain cells (neurons) needed for this process exist in their billions at birth, they only have the *potential* for functioning. Until they connect up with other neurons to form pathways they cannot affect behaviour or thought, and if they are unused they die (a process known as apoptosis).

Building neural pathways is a 'use it or lose it' mechanism that leading researcher and therapist Margot Sunderland has termed 'brain sculpting', and it is parents who do the sculpting. Repeated interaction with your baby stimulates the formation of these pathways by prompting neurons to fire their way through the brain, joining up with each other to create these important, complex pathways. In fact,

CORTISOL

This so-called stress hormone is released by young babies in times of distress and anxiety. With comfort and reassurance, levels fall. If a baby's levels are often high, he becomes less able to regulate cortisol production and less resilient to life's buffeting. In some cases, a baby protects himself by shutting down cortisol production and not expressing distress at all. He becomes passive and less able to respond to social and emotional overtures and to enjoy the happier aspects of life.

these essential neural connections depend solely on experience. If the right experience doesn't happen, then the connections simply don't get made, and the brain's size and functions are permanently reduced.

Your baby's biochemical production also enables normal brain development. When two humans touch each other gently and kindly, oxytocin – sometimes called the love hormone – is produced in both of them. When one of them is a baby, repeated oxytocin production helps activate the neural connections and pathways of the brain in a positive way. On the other hand, if a baby is allowed to feel fear or distress, without any calming, his body is flooded with stress hormones, such as cortisol, which he is unable to process – and the hard-wiring that takes place in the brain risks being set to 'alarm', with no way of turning it down. Future events and stimulations similar to the events that caused him to feel fearful and abandoned may produce an over-reaction. In practical terms, the baby who is loved, responded to, physically held and cuddled, and whose distress is regarded as something that needs attention and calming, is one whose social brain develops *normally*.

Healthy brain development is supported by the species-specific ingredients contained in breast milk. Moreover, when breastfeeding is going well it is easier to create the necessary and repeated closeness and responsiveness that lead to positive neural pathways developing in the brain. If you are feeding your baby by bottle – whether it's formula or expressed breast milk – you will need to create similar warm and loving experiences (see pages 98–9).

Emotional needs

First developed in the 1960s and '70s, but with earlier roots, 'attachment theory' is a well-researched, robustly evidenced and testable scientific theory concerned with the relationships between human beings.

When it relates to infancy, attachment looks at the early connections between babies and their prime carers. It describes the basic need of babies to find love, attention and closeness, and how achieving this forms an important 'internal working model', or a sort of template, for future relationships. Theorists went on to identify different forms of attachment – such as secure, avoidant, anxious, disorganised, resistant – and these categories are still being developed and used to explore, and to treat, difficulties in relationships at other stages of life.

In the past 20 years or so, attachment theory – which comes from an essentially psychodynamic, psychoanalytical area of study (to do with unseen processes of the mind) – has been strongly supported and extended by our greater technical understanding of neurology, the study of brain development. Detailed

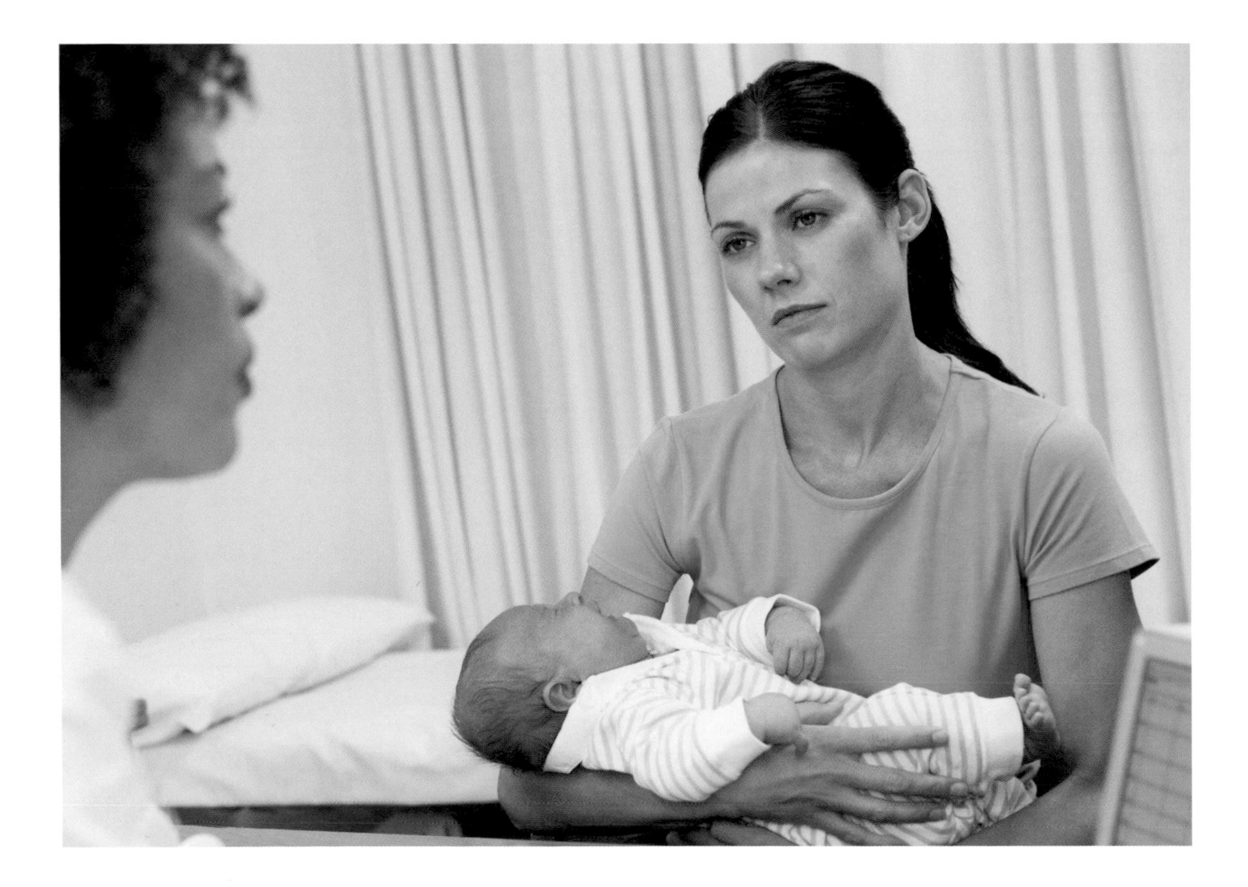

scanning techniques now make it possible to see how emotion and feeling operate in the brain.

At the same time, science has shown how the biochemistry of emotional response works on the way we function. For example, we now know how stress levels prompt chemical production, which in turn affects the brain and the body, and how pleasure hormones work when we exchange loving gestures and touches.

'Bonding' is a term that was first used in the 1970s. While it's sometimes used interchangeably with attachment, bonding has more to do with the mother relating to her baby, while attachment focuses on the baby relating to his mother. Initially, studies seemed to indicate that there was a crucial post-birth time for bonding to happen, and that if it didn't happen then, it was somehow too late. We now know more about this: the immediate post-birth period can be a wonderfully rich, loving episode for mother and baby (and fathers, too) with a great deal of sensory exchange (see page 56), and we know mothers and babies should not be physically separated in the early hours and days unless medically necessary. But attachment and bonding are processes, not events; they can certainly start at birth (or even before) but they don't actually depend on everything being in place at that time.

It's clear that our emotional and social lives, understanding and mental wellbeing begin in babyhood – and with responsive, loving parenting. This development is supported by breastfeeding – or by formula feeding that re-creates some of the emotional environment of breastfeeding – and we'll see later how this is done (page 55).

Factors affecting attachment

Many women (and some men) experience some form of mental or emotional distress before and/or after the arrival of a new baby and this can affect bonding and attachment with their baby.

HOW SURE ARE WE THAT ATTACHMENT MATTERS?

There is no controversy about the importance of attachment. What we don't fully know, however, is exactly how much different forms of attachment have an impact on future development, and how directly attachment causes different outcomes later in life. You can describe attachment, and its different types, but it can't be measured in centimetres or kilograms, and nor can its effects. However, we do know that attachment is a vital part of how everyone grows and develops as a person.

After basic physical survival, it's the most important part of babyhood – and our own experience of attachment as babies and children can have an impact on what sort of parents we become.

This is sometimes labelled postnatal or perinatal (the time around birth, and including pregnancy) depression, but the word 'depression' is something of a catch-all. There are several different forms of postnatal/perinatal mental illness; mothers may be anxious or stressed and may even suffer post-traumatic stress disorder. In rare cases (one or two in every 1,000), pregnancy and birth may precede puerperal psychosis (see box) – disturbed and disturbing behaviour where the mother loses touch with reality. In addition, other forms of mental distress, like bipolar disorder or schizophrenia, can happen postnatally, just as at any other time.

Ways to beat the blues

- Don't try and do too much; leave non-vital chores for later or ask others to do them.
- Nap whenever you can.
- Try some relaxation techniques such as meditation.
- Get out and about.
- Join a new mothers' support group.
- Make time to do things that make you laugh.
- Treat yourself well; don't force yourself to do things that upset you or make you feel stressed.

Baby blues

In the first days after birth, it's very common to be affected by a tearful, low mood, which lasts a few days at most. It could be related to a 'coming down' after the high of giving birth; sleep deprivation and rapid hormone shifts are other contributing factors. If you experience the blues, no real treatment is needed, though it helps if the people around you are sympathetic and patient, show care and concern, and offer you support.

Stay close to your baby during this time and respond to his feeding cues. The first week after birth can be overwhelming for some women, and being worried that they're not doing things right or that the baby is not feeding enough or feeding too much or not effectively adds to the stress. Your midwife should be able to let you know the signs that things are perfectly normal, and suggest ways to help if they are not.

Postnatal depression

A low mood, which is longer lasting and stronger in its effects than the baby blues, is termed postnatal depression.

Research shows that 10–15 per cent of new mothers are depressed after the birth, and there may be many more who have weeks or months of intermittent low mood. Depression may begin in pregnancy and this, along with other forms of mental and emotional disturbance such as anxiety, is a risk factor for postnatal depression.

Negative feelings are a continuum or spectrum, with the most severe collection of symptoms affecting a woman all day, every day at one end, and temporary spells of feeling low, or isolated or very tired at the other end. Some researchers feel it is misleading to have a cut-off

PUERPERAL PSYCHOSIS

This is a serious mental illness, which usually shows up in the first week or so after birth. It's usually obvious to anyone that something is not right – a mother with puerperal psychosis may have delusions and extreme mood swings as well as bouts of extreme physical activity at odd times of the day or night. Hospital treatment is usually required.

point, where some women are depressed and other women are not. The term 'dysphoria' has been suggested to describe this low mood rather than the more clinically specific depression.

Whatever the correct term, 'postnatal depression' is used to describe the experience of prolonged, serious, negative feelings after a birth – even if they actually began during pregnancy, and are not necessarily depression, but anxiety, obsession or stress.

If you experience serious tiredness, difficulty sleeping, tearfulness, strong fears and worries that you are not coping as well as others, you need to consider whether you are suffering from postnatal depression. If you are, it's important to get help, not just for your sake, but for that of your baby, too.

Babies of mothers with prolonged mental distress have an increased risk of social, learning and behavioural problems, which may be long lasting. Moreover, a depressed mother is less able to relate to and respond to her baby and, in such cases, an attachment disorder is common.

In recent years, it's become more accepted that men can suffer postnatal mental illness as well – a recent study of more than 8,000 fathers in the UK found that eight weeks after the birth, one in 25 was suffering from postnatal depression. This compares with one in 10 mothers. There is a slightly higher risk if a man's partner is already having problems, but it can occur independently. Men, however, are less likely to ask for help than women. A depressed father has a serious negative impact on normal family relationships. It has been suggested that boys in particular will suffer as sons appear to be influenced from a very early age by the behaviour of their fathers.

Getting help

If you suspect you (or your partner) may be suffering postnatal problems, speak to your doctor, midwife or health visitor – and be honest. You might be given a questionnaire aimed at assessing whether or not you need more investigation for postnatal depression.

Medication including antidepressants is one option, and there are antidepressants that are safe to take when breastfeeding. Some women are helped by being referred for counselling and/or psychotherapy on its own or in combination with antidepressants. In less severe cases, getting out a bit more and going to places where there is support and friendship can help.

In some areas you can be referred to a specialist infant mental health service if it's suspected that your baby may be affected by your mental or emotional state.

Other barriers to attachment

We can be pretty certain that for most of human existence, mothers and babies stayed close together. The infant brain and body were formed in this environment – for the baby, his environment was his mother. This is the biological, physiological norm for babies, who certainly don't know they are born in the 21st century and are thought better off in a cot or pram, feeding at predictable, regular intervals.

Unrestricted proximity fosters attachment best and anything that keeps mothers and babies apart is a challenge to attachment. While in most cases, this is not insurmountable, it may still be a barrier. If you and your baby have to be separated at birth because of health issues (perhaps because your baby needs to spend some time in special care), you should get together as soon and as often as possible.

Moreover, if, as a new mother you are told by a healthcare worker or a relative, or read in a book, or you simply have an expectation that your baby should be held and fed at pre-ordained times, you need to know that you can do something different. Simply allow your baby and yourself to find a responsive and mutually happy pattern that works.

Also, if you are not able to breastfeed, or find your baby is unable to do so effectively, or for whatever reason you choose not to, you can make a conscious decision to stay in close physical contact when you offer a bottle and be the one who gives the most feeds.

Getting the proximity underway, from the start, is a very good way of overcoming all those interferences – and helps mothers and babies fall in love with each other. Fathers, too, can foster attachment in this way, as can other people who are close to your baby. Babies cannot attach to more than one or two main people at first – these intense, early relationships allow them to have confidence and trust in others as they get a little older.

Fathers who are involved in their babies' care right from the start become strongly attached to them, developing their own relationship which may be different from, but as nurturing as, a mother's.

FIRST YEAR MILESTONES

'Milestones' is the popular term for recognised stages of development, which healthy growing babies reach at predictable ages, usually in a predictable order. Physical milestones are divided into two categories known as 'gross' and 'fine' motor skills. 'Gross' refers to the skills that enable your baby to move, roll, sit up, cruise round furniture, crawl and walk. These allow him to gain an understanding of the world from increasingly varied angles. 'Fine' motor skills are the movements he makes with his arms, hands and fingers to touch, hold, examine and explore, furthering his learning and understanding. There are also measurable mental, sensory, social and emotional milestones. These non-physical milestone are intimately linked to your baby's physical growth and abilities.

Each area of development supports other areas. Your baby wants to hold a rattle and reach a ball or touch your face and play with your hair; his need to do these things is irresistible and his emotional urge to do them supports his physical capabilities. He wants to do them just when he starts to be able to do them, showing how emotional and physical developments work in tandem.

By the end of the time spans listed here, your baby will probably show these aspects of social development – and many more, too. The following two pages offer an overview of milestones related to your baby's social, emotional and cognitive (learning and understanding) development, plus their links with feeding.

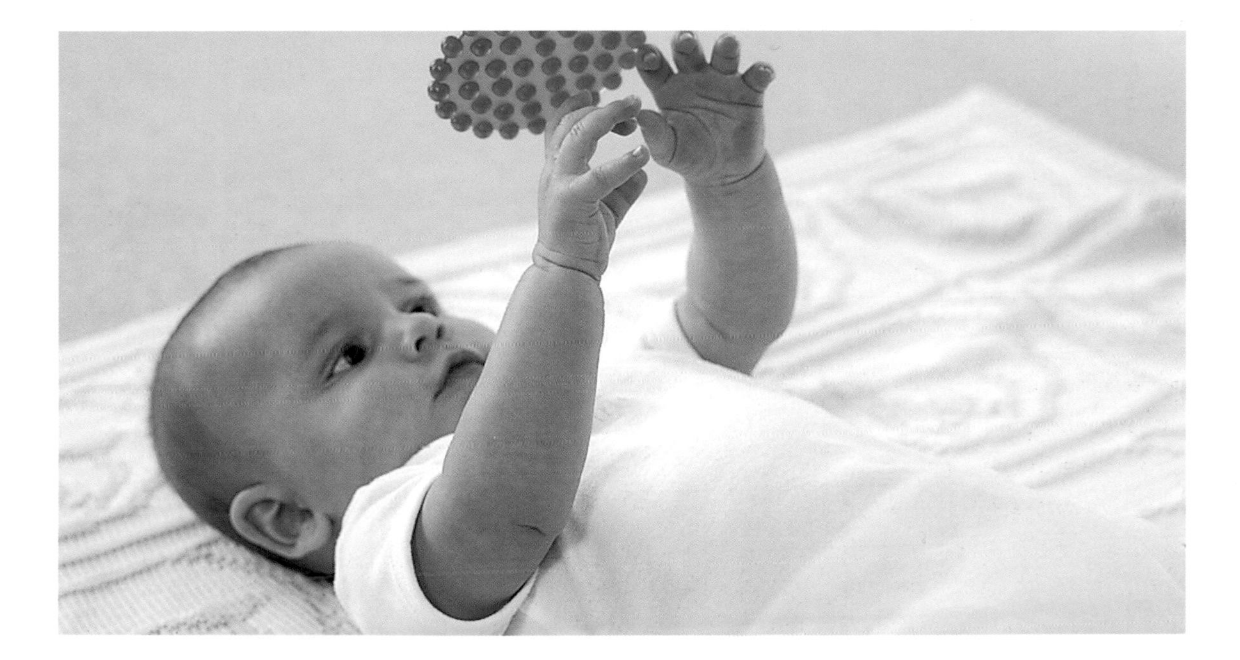

Month 1

Your baby responds to eye contact and prefers to look at faces, especially those of people he knows. He may show by the expression on his face and in turning his head that he recognises familiar voices. When he's calm, and feeling satisfied after a feed or perhaps having a short break mid-feed, he's likely to fix his gaze on your face and may mimic your facial expressions. His 'feeding cues' include hand waving, facial movements, and sounds which start as squeaks and may move up the scale to cries.

Month 2

Your baby smiles in response to you, and smiles to convey pleasure and engagement. His gurglings and cooings have the shape of speech, with gaps and stops and starts, and you can have a 'conversation' with him. Indeed, he may break off sucking and swallowing in order to seek out your face and focus on it, and to have a 'chat'.

Month 3

Your baby laughs and giggles with delight; he smiles spontaneously when he hears your voice. He shows his excitement and engagement when he knows he is going to be fed.

Month 4

Your baby's attention is grabbed by moving objects and he tries to reach out for something he likes. He shows by his behaviour and delight that the people closest to him are his favourites and clearly discriminates between those he loves and those he doesn't know. If he is bottlefed, he may show he does not want to be fed by someone unfamiliar to him. Breast- or bottlefed, he can be distracted by the sound of someone's voice or someone coming into the room, and he pulls away in order to investigate.

Month 5

Your baby can enjoy playing 'peek-a-boo'; he loves to see himself in the mirror (though he does not yet understand that the baby in the mirror and he are the same person). He can hold objects and examine textures. When feeding, he may like to touch and hold your hand, or play with your clothing, or pat your skin – and if you're wearing a necklace, watch out or make sure it's firmly strung!

Month 6

Your baby can clearly express emotions in his face and voice – joy, displeasure, fear, anticipation or worry. If he is not interested in feeding at that time, he fully understands the message he communicates by pushing the bottle away, or pulling himself away from you.

Month 7

Your baby understands that if something is dropped, or falls, it still exists – and he will look for it. This is a big step – it shows he has grasped there is a world outside what he can immediately see, feel and hear. He can babble and make consonant sounds (like 'ba-ba-ba' and 'ma-ma-ma'). He shows he understands that breasts exist under clothing by patting or holding your clothes when he wants to feed. If he's using a cup, he's getting to know that liquid is often inside it, even when he can't see it.

Month 8

Your baby can show by his reactions that he knows when something is going to happen. So, the sound of a key in the door and the door opening can mean 'daddy's home!'. Getting out his highchair or bib means 'mealtime', and he'll show anticipation and pleasure.

Month 9

Your baby may show separation anxiety and object strongly when you leave the room, but calm down when you return. He gets upset if you remove a toy from his hands. He lifts his arms to signal to you he wants to be picked up. He can hand you his cup or bottle when he wants more to drink. If you're breastfeeding and you return home after some time away, he may welcome you with joy and 'reconnect' with you through a breastfeed.

Month 10

Your baby can understand 'no' and may even shake his head as if he knows this means 'no' as well, though he might equally well nod! He enjoys 'reading' a book with you and knows that if he turns a page, something new will appear. If he rejects the offer of a bottle or a breastfeed, he may shake his head as well as pushing the bottle (or you) away. He may do the same with food he doesn't like.

Month 11

Your baby can 'pretend play' by combing dolly's hair, or cuddling and kissing teddy. He understands that playing 'having a cup of tea' in the bath is not real – and he'll laugh at the game.

Month 12

Your baby begins to use 'protodeclarative pointing' – that is, he uses his index finger, or perhaps his whole hand, to draw attention to something that's caught his eye. This is a powerful piece of communication, which your baby uses to share his experiences with you as well as to get his needs met. He may point to a familiar item in the supermarket – 'Look, Mummy, that's what I eat at home!' is his message.

Note: This is a rough guide only. Babies develop skills at different speeds: some will be quicker than others in acquiring all skills while others may make faster progress with motor skills than social or mental skills.

CHAPTER 2

Breastfeeding today

Across the world, breastfeeding has declined over the past 100 years or so, with a more rapid drop in the second half of the 20th century. The contributing factors include an increase in the marketing of infant formula milk and various changes in society. In Western societies, today's smaller families and our less communal way of living mean breastfeeding is literally not seen as much. This means that the skills and knowledge that make breastfeeding work have to be rediscovered, rather than being passed on through the generations and learnt by observation and just being around people who do it.

Some of the aspects of breastfeeding affected by modern-day life are outlined in this chapter, as are some of the newer discoveries that have led to a greater understanding of breast milk and breastfeeding.

A brief look back

Human life emerged about 200,000 years ago, and throughout that time the vast majority of babies have been breastfed. In *The Politics of Breastfeeding* (2009), author Gabrielle Palmer states 'Most humans who have walked this earth never drank a drop of non-human milk.'

Anthropologists studying the pre-industrial societies that still exist in our own age observe that infants breastfeed well into middle childhood. Dr Katherine Dettwyler (an American anthropologist at the University of Delaware) has calculated that the natural time, in physiological terms, for weaning from the breast is between two-and-a-half and seven years. She calculates this from what we know of the way other mammals, including other primates, grow; the weight at which other mammals wean; the eruption of permanent teeth and other factors; and from what she observed in the field, working in Mali, where no one breastfeeds according to a clock, but rather according to a child's expressed need.

However, breastfeeding involves a social set of behaviours, and as soon as human beings start relating to each other and influencing the way each other lives, other factors come into play.

Breastfeeding has not been universal in every society. In fact, some mothers throughout time and in all cultures have deliberately not breastfed at all. This was not necessarily a 'choice' made by mothers – who in most societies were pretty powerless – but a reflection of prevalent ideas, which they were obliged to follow, whether or not they could think of any alternatives. Not all cultures have put much value on mothering; in some, there was very little concern and consideration for infant welfare.

Wet nursing – babies being breastfed by women other than their own mothers – was prevalent in many societies across many cultures. Typically, wet nurses were from a lower class than the mother; sometimes, they were servants or even slaves. The ancient Roman elite used slaves in this way, and there are examples throughout recorded history of wet nursing among the higher social classes through to the end of the 19th century. Born in 1874, Winston Churchill was wet nursed as were Queen Victoria's nine children in the 1840s and 1850s. Victoria herself regarded breastfeeding with horror (and she wasn't too keen on pregnancy and childbirth either, though her diaries and letters make it clear she enjoyed sex, so this was not a general 'Victorian' prudishness about bodily matters). She was shocked and scornful when two of her daughters, Alice and Vicky, elected to breastfeed their own children themselves.

In some countries, including Britain, throughout the 18th and 19th centuries, 'baby farms' existed for children of all classes; infants were sent away to be nursed shortly after birth and did not return until toddlerhood (there were also several baby farming scandals, where babies died from neglect).

It was, however, always known that non-breastfed babies were at greater risk of illness and death and that breastfeeding prevented pregnancy and protected maternal health. In 17th-century England, for example, it's been shown that upper-class women who did not breastfeed experienced serial pregnancies, many accompanied by life-threatening gynaecological and obstetrical problems alongside high rates of miscarriage, stillbirth and infant mortality. In contrast, poor (or at least not rich) mothers who breastfed had fewer children who were more robust; these mothers had easier pregnancies and labours, too. Rich women, unlike their simpler-living counterparts, were thought to be too delicate to breastfeed and were not expected to indulge in such 'animal-like' behaviour.

In Europe, from the start of the 19th century the Industrial Revolution began to have its effects and women started working in factories. Unlike farm workers or women who worked in cottage industries, factory workers couldn't take time off to care for their babies, or fit in breastfeeding around their work, so babies were weaned off the breast quickly, or fed to a schedule that allowed their mothers to work.

Over the past 100 years or so, thoughts on infant and child health and welfare and women's wellbeing (physical, mental, economic, social, marital) have evolved and these are now considered worthy of protection, at least in the West. At the same time, industrial and economic changes have allowed the mass production of breastfeeding substitutes (bottles, teats, formula milks, baby foods), which have brought comparatively safe artificial feeding within the means of just about everyone.

Commercial activity promoting breastfeeding substitutes has undermined breastfeeding in many ways, but in the last 30 years or so knowledge of how breastfeeding works has become more science based, and it's become increasingly clear that breastfeeding brings with it several measurable health benefits.

Over the same recent period, maternity ward practices have also changed to encourage breastfeeding. The vast majority of babies are born in hospital, and for decades institutional rules about scheduled feeding and the routine separation of mothers and babies worked against the establishment of successful breastfeeding. Even those mothers who chose to breastfeed found it a miserably ineffective way of nourishing their babies: breastfeeding simply does not work if night feeds are banned, if mothers are not allowed to feed more often than every four hours, and if infant feeding cues are not followed. The Baby Friendly Initiative (see page 144) was, and remains, an important counter to these practices.

In the UK, breastfeeding hit a low in the late 1960s and early '70s, but by the 1980s, surveys showed that the decline had ceased. Now, in the early 21st century, surveys show that 76 per cent of women begin to feed their babies at the breast. Too many, however, stop in the first days and weeks, because of a lack of the support and information they need to sustain them in this choice.

Understanding the research

The large number of medical and social studies that look at infant feeding continue to confirm that in all cultures and societies how you feed your baby makes a difference to the health and wellbeing of both you and your baby.

Such studies consider how, for example, such things as health, growth, physical and mental wellbeing, relationships, survival itself, hospital admissions, doctor's visits, school performance and behaviour are influenced by feeding. Researchers find out about feeding by looking at written records, asking carers to remember, or by tracking babies as they grow and asking the question at each observation session or interview. They then look at the aspect of health, growth and so on they're investigating.

Not all studies get their information in the same way, or look at the same numbers of babies or even offer reliable conclusions. How confident can you be that the conclusions can tell you about other babies, ones not in the study? Does the study actually add to the knowledge about infant feeding and babies in general?

A study may challenge existing knowledge, by bringing up a surprising result, or contradict previous studies, and sometimes a later study throws light on a puzzling or unclear set of outcomes from a previous study.

Examples of this exist in the research into breastfeeding and intelligence. Some studies show no apparent difference in intelligence between formula-fed babies and breastfed babies; other studies show a difference of several IQ points. Controlling for confounding variables (see box, right) and assessing intelligence (or even defining intelligence) are not easy, so in one way, it's not surprising results are contradictory.

Recent research reported the discovery that nine out of ten babies possess a gene which allows them to use the brain-boosting fatty acids in breast milk, resulting in better IQ performance. The fact that other breastfeeding studies have not investigated this gene (because it was not known about at the time) could explain the differences in results. Interestingly, none of the studies comparing breastfeeding outcomes with formula feeding outcomes show that formula feeding increases intelligence.

A BEGINNER'S GUIDE TO CHECKING OUT THE RESEARCH

Take a topical example of an outcome that might be associated with the way babies are fed – obesity. It's often said that formula-fed babies have a higher risk of becoming obese children than breastfed babies. A lower risk of obesity is often cited as one of the benefits of breastfeeding. A study could simply count the number of obese children in a group of a certain age and see how many were breastfed and how many were formula fed. This would show that obese children are more likely to have been formula fed, suggesting a connection. Alternatively, a 'cohort' – a selected group of subjects – could be recruited and followed to see which ones are obese at, say, age six. The same result will appear – there will be more obese children within the numbers who were formula fed.

However, neither result proves that formula feeding causes obesity. It could be, for example, that these obese children came from families whose lifestyles or behaviours make obesity in their children more likely, and that these families are also more likely to select formula feeding than breastfeeding. So the study would reveal a difference between families, not between feeding choices. The formula-fed babies would be expected to have a higher risk of obesity not because of how they were fed but because they come from families with an existing heightened risk of obesity.

A different approach was used in a German study of almost 10,000 children that looked at whether infant feeding made a difference to their risk of obesity. To make sure they were comparing feeding method, and not families, the researchers accounted for (or controlled) several confounding variables (a term that means other factors, which vary between subjects of the study and which could confuse the results). The study concluded that formula feeding did increase the risk of obesity and overweight at school entry, but it was only one of a number of factors.

Breastfeeding was found to be a protective factor against obesity and overweight. The researchers found a 'dose-response' effect, with more breastfeeding being associated with less overweight.

The UK's Millennium Cohort Study (MCS) looked at 19,000 babies born around 2000. In addition to information about the babies' feeding, researchers tracked individual babies to find out which ones needed hospital treatment for diarrhoeal and respiratory infection in the first eight months of life. Formula feeding increased the risk of hospitalisation.

This effect persisted even when social and economic factors were taken into account – it was clear from the results that it was the feeding method that made the difference to the babies' risk of illness.

More than just milk

Human milk is more than just the sum of its parts. When its constituents are analysed and measured, it becomes clear that many of its properties work in harmony. Some may be involved not so much in nourishing a baby, but in regulating milk production and in enhancing the experience of breastfeeding by inducing feelings of calm and closeness between mother and baby.

Human breast milk is biologically specific, that is, it is made up of ingredients that are suited to the needs of a human infant. We can be confident that the amount of ingredient X or Y matches a baby's precise requirements, at the very time she requires them. Human milk varies from mother to mother, and changes according to the time of day, the age of the baby and her appetite. These variations allow the breast milk to include specific infection-fighting antibodies (see below).

Scientifically speaking, breast milk consists mainly of water (about 88 per cent). The bulkiest nutrients in it (per 100 ml) are:

- Lactose (milk sugars) 7.0 g
- Fat 4.2 g
- Protein 1.3 g.

The energy (calorie) content of breast milk is about 70 kcal per 100 ml. In addition to sodium and iron, milk also contains many other minerals, vitamins and trace elements. These ingredients are, broadly speaking, vital to a baby's growth and nutrition. They're easily accessed and digested by the baby's system, and they're uniquely human. Other mammals' milks may contain the same basic ingredients but, understandably, they are not the same as human milk.

Protecting your baby

Perhaps greater than a baby's need to grow is her need to be protected from aspects of her environment which could make her ill. The immunity-boosting properties of breast milk can help your baby remain in good health by helping her combat infection and reducing the risk of allergy.

Breast milk contains proteins called immunoglobulins: these are antibodies that act on undesirable molecules (or pathogens) in the immune system, including bacteria and viruses. Along with specific types of white blood cells – phagocytes and lymphocytes – the immunoglobulins support your baby's developing immunity by mopping up agents that cause infection.

When a pathogen enters a baby's body through her skin or saliva, she has specific antibodies to fight it. A mother makes antibodies to fight infection in her gut, and passes them on to her baby through her blood and milk. The antibodies have a biochemical 'shield' which protects them from being destroyed in the baby's gut.

Other protective factors present in breast milk include lactobacilli, so-called friendly bacteria, which promote gut health, and oligosaccharides, sugars that can be important in preventing allergy.

The process is important

Breastfeeding and breast milk work dynamically, that is, the process is based on mother and baby working together. Breastfeeding succeeds best in nourishing a baby when it is done unrestrictedly and responsively, so it matches a baby's needs, appetite and normal desire for closeness and comforting. When breastfeeding is going well, the behaviours associated with it promote attachment and bonding, and make it easier to ensure happy, healthy relationships.

Nutrients in the milk – principally long-chain unsaturated fatty acids – support a baby's brain development and complement the changes taking place there in response to her social environment, that is, her relationships with the people around her (see pages 12–13).

Breastfeeding is something mothers and babies enjoy together, when a baby cues it. A baby feeds according to her appetite and needs, slowing down to reduce her intake when she's had enough, so her needs control the quantity she takes. While being fed, she is held closely, her skin against your skin, so that her senses of touch, smell and sight are stimulated. She gets a warm drink that changes flavour subtly, because some of the flavours in your diet come through, so her taste buds are stimulated. She comes to relate to her primary carer – her mother – and that helps lay the template for all future relationships. Breastfeeding makes it easy for this to happen, without much conscious effort on your part – as long as you go with the flow and allow it to happen.

Support for breastfeeding

Over the past 50 years or so, various organisations have developed in many countries with the aim of protecting breastfeeding and supporting individual breastfeeding mothers and babies.

BOTTLEFEEDING CONSIDERATIONS

The experience of formula feeding is obviously different from breastfeeding in terms of how the milk gets to your baby. However, you and your baby can still experience the closeness, connection and intimacy of breastfeeding – experiences mothers often say they miss when they switch to formula – even if breastfeeding has not gone well for you.

Your formula-fed baby also needs gentle, comforting and close handling while being fed and to build up her confidence and familiarity with the experience you share with her (see page 98).

She needs to learn, too, that when she shows signs of wanting to feed, her needs will be met lovingly and reliably. If you are formula feeding, you can aim to be just as responsive to early feeding cues with the bottle – mouthing and fussing – as you would be with the breast.

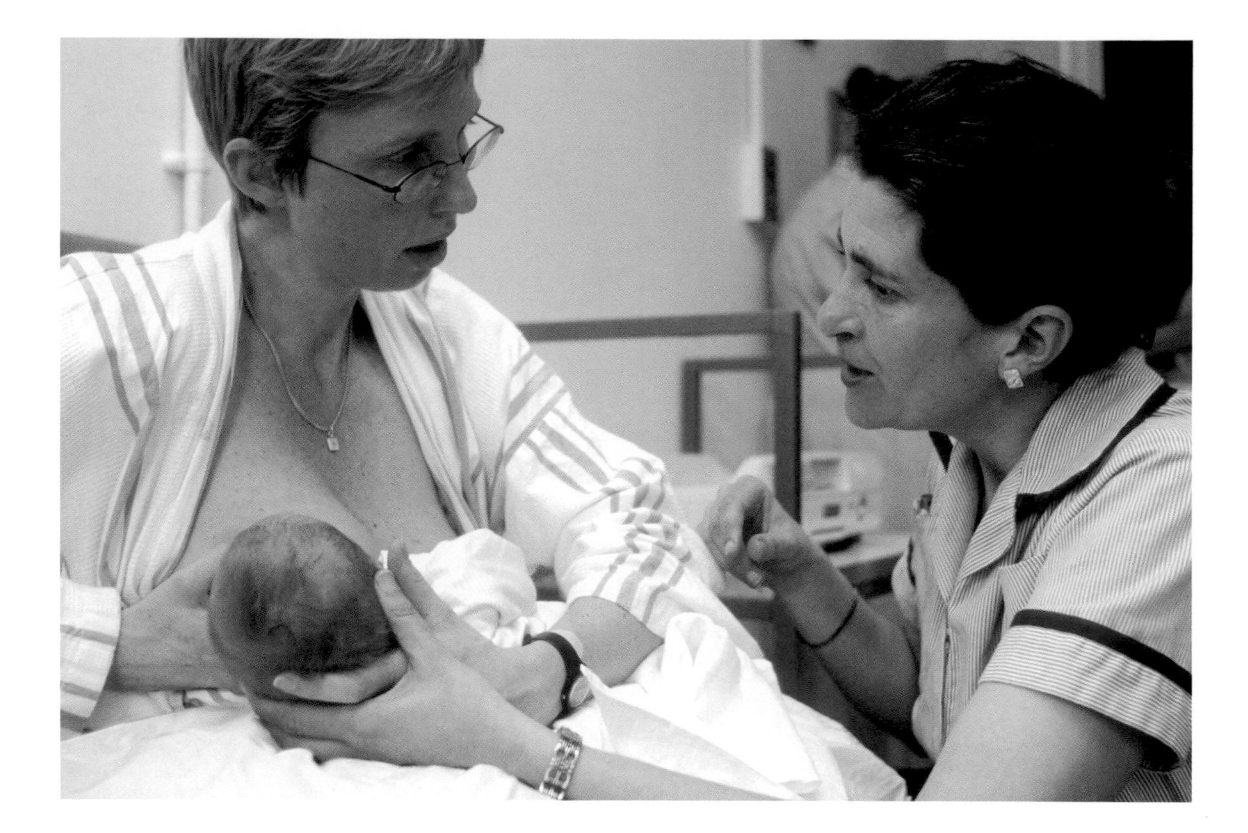

This has happened as a result of a growing awareness that the skills needed to ensure happy, comfortable breastfeeding can't survive by themselves. Breastfeeding has become something women have to actively choose to do and they can't rely on those closest to them to know what to do to make it succeed. They may also come up against healthcare practices that either don't help or, worse, undermine them.

The first mother-led movement to support breastfeeding was La Leche League, which began in the USA in the late 1950s. La Leche League – 'la leche' (pronounced 'la laychay') is Spanish for 'the milk' – spread across the world, and now there are very few places where you can't find help at the end of a phone from a trained LLL leader, and a group where you can meet other breastfeeding mothers. La Leche League leaders are volunteers, and their training involves counselling skills and knowledge of breastfeeding. Many countries have various organisations and networks of their own.

While you are in hospital, support for breastfeeding is on hand but it doesn't stop once you leave. Health visitors and breastfeeding counsellors are a phone call or a visit away and can offer advice and encouragement if it's not going well.

In the UK, there are a number of other mother-led volunteer organisations, which train women in similar ways, with a focus on non-judgemental support. La Leche League (Great Britain), the Association of Breastfeeding Mothers and the Breastfeeding Network (BfN) all have telephone helplines, websites and local groups.

The National Childbirth Trust is Britain's largest parenting charity, concerned with pregnancy, birth and early parenthood. Its trained, volunteer breastfeeding counsellors teach antenatal sessions on breastfeeding, support individual women postnatally and run breastfeeding support groups. They, too, have telephone helplines, a website and local groups.

In the past decade, in some areas of the UK and elsewhere peer supporters have been trained to offer friendship, social support and basic breastfeeding knowledge to women in their own communities. International Board Certified Lactation Consultants (IBCLCs) have qualified for the status, and may be in private practice. In the UK, they are often healthcare professionals or volunteer breastfeeding counsellors as well.

If you need to talk to someone about breastfeeding, then contact the organisations and telephone lines listed on page 144.

CAMPAIGNS AND PROGRAMMES

Hospitals and healthcare professionals generally encourage breastfeeding, but maternity care practices have not always been helpful. Challenging that is the worldwide Baby Friendly Initiative, from UNICEF (United Nations Children's Fund), which is well established internationally. The initiative helps hospitals improve their care of mothers and babies and assesses them to award 'Baby Friendly' status. The programme, based on good evidence, makes sure maternity services don't separate mothers and babies, give any unnecessary formula (unless the mother makes an informed choice to do so) and that mothers who use formula are aware of safe ways to prepare it.

The World Health Organisation (WHO) and UNICEF have jointly developed a Global Strategy for Infant and Young Child Feeding, which gives information to governments on the legislation and public health measures needed to protect breastfeeding.

Many individual countries, at national and local government level, have policies and programmes on infant feeding. The professional and educational bodies of many healthcare professions – midwives, doctors in all their guises and specialisms, nurses, dietitians – have statements, policies or guidelines for their members' professional practice.

Internationally, the International Baby Food Action Network (IBFAN) is the umbrella organisation. The British-based Baby Milk Action is a member (see page 144).

Working and breastfeeding

The majority of women expect to continue, or to return, to work while their children are young. The best family-friendly legislation, employment practice and social security systems recognise this and give women the option of working as a genuine choice. A genuine choice, however, should not have to mean leaving your baby with other carers too soon, or for too long, and it should not mean a curtailment of breastfeeding.

If your baby is six months or more at the time you return to work, things will be relatively straightforward. If you can, it's helpful to wait to go back to work until then for several reasons:

- Your baby will not rely on breastfeeding for all her nutritional needs: she can have some solid food.
- With help at first, your baby will be able to use a cup for drinks – useful if she has never had a bottle, or if she objects to using one.
- You will have passed the stage when missing breastfeeds would make you feel very uncomfortable and at risk of engorgement or, worse, mastitis (see page 81). Note: you will be uncomfortable at first, but this will pass after a few days.

Your choices for your baby's nutrition will depend on her age and the length of time you spend away from her. If your baby is older and well established on solid foods, she may be fine with no breast milk at all during the time you are away – she can have other fluids if needed – and you can breastfeed her in the morning, evening, at night and when you're not working. This solution is particularly easy if you work part time. Often, this is a matter of your own judgement and common sense and practicality, rather than a set of certainties you can apply to your own individual baby. Talk it over with your health visitor or doctor, a nutritionist or a breastfeeding counsellor.

If you can stay at home with your baby for longer, or you can be flexible for longer, then so much the better. (See page 84 for information on longer periods of breastfeeding and working.)

AN EARLY RETURN?

The sooner after the birth you start to work away from your baby, the more challenging it is to maintain your milk supply and your comfort. Nevertheless, it can be done.

You will need to express at work, at least as often as you'd expect your baby to feed, and your baby will need to learn to take the milk from a bottle; babies of less than six months can use a cup if it's held for them. You'll need somewhere clean, safe and private to express, and somewhere clean and safe to store your milk.

For information about expressing and storing breast milk, see pages 106–7.

Environmental hazards

In our polluted world it is inevitable that contaminants find their way into breast milk. Persistent organic pollutants (POPs), which include substances like dioxin, polychlorinated biphenyls (PCBs), pesticides and other chemicals, are found in soil, and from there they reach many of the foods we eat, and enter the water we drink and the air we breathe.

We accumulate these contaminants in our fatty tissues and elsewhere, and they are part of the environment we create for our babies in pregnancy. As a mother's fat stores are involved in the production of breast milk, these contaminants can be passed on during breastfeeding. Is this something to be worried about? Should we somehow work out a way of purifying ourselves and our milk, or even avoid breastfeeding altogether in favour of formula?

Currently, it's virtually impossible to differentiate any potential breastfeeding-related effects of pollutants from any results of growing inside the uterus and being nourished by the mother's blood supply (which contains the same contaminants) there. While the in-utero exposure to these contaminants is smaller than during breastfeeding, a developing fetus is likely to be more vulnerable to them because of the rapid growth and cell division taking place during gestation.

It's a good idea to minimise exposure to avoidable contaminants. However, a true reduction of pollution in our environment can only happen as a result of national and international initiatives, which is beyond the scope of this book to explore.

There is no evidence at all that formula could be a better option. Formula milk comes from cows living in the same environment, and the milk powder is then reconstituted with water from the same environment, and delivered through plastic bottles and silicone or latex teats. The green option is certainly breastfeeding.

BREASTFEEDING MYTHS

Modern concerns about breastfeeding have translated into misbeliefs, fallacies and dire warnings, many of which are just not true. Here are just some of those you might hear.

Breastfeeding makes your breasts sag.

There is no difference in sagging between women who have breastfed and those who have not.

Neither my mum nor her sister had enough milk; I'm bound to have problems.

There's no evidence that milk supply is inherited. The main thing affecting the amount of milk available is whether your baby feeds often and effectively enough. Previous generations of mothers may not have had the knowledge, or the support, to allow this.

There's not really any difference between breast milk and formula these days.

Modern formulas are largely the same as they have always been, despite minor changes over the past 20 years or so. They are based on cows' milk and there will always be differences because of that.

You have to have a healthy diet in order to breastfeed – and you need to drink plenty of water as well.

While it's a good idea to eat a healthy diet and be sufficiently hydrated, the quality and quantity of breast milk is largely unaffected by the food the mother eats. Drinking to quench thirst is quite sufficient, though sometimes mothers feel thirstier when breastfeeding.

A mother needs to rest a lot when breastfeeding.

Breastfeeding is no more tiring than formula feeding, and the amount of rest or sleep a mother has impacts on her own wellbeing but not on her breastfeeding.

You can't drink alcohol and breastfeed.

This is untrue unless you overdo things, become drunk and/or are unable to care for your baby. Alcohol does reach breast milk in very small amounts, but an occasional drink is not considered damaging. Alcohol is processed by your body at the rate of one unit every one to two hours. Although it passes out of your milk freely, when it is no longer present in your bloodstream, it is no longer present in your milk.

Breastfeeding takes up more time than formula feeding.

While it is true that breastfed babies may feed more often than formula-fed babies, you save time by not buying equipment and formula, preparing the feed and washing and sterilising equipment between feeds. The time spent actually feeding varies, but once breastfeeding is established, many breastfed babies feed quickly and efficiently. Night feeds are typically a lot quicker with breastfed babies too.

Breastfeeding hurts – especially when a baby has teeth!

Breastfeeding should always be comfortable for you; if it isn't, get help (see pages 65 and 144). Teeth make no difference, as a baby doesn't use her teeth to suck.

Breastfeeding means no one else can bond with the baby.

Breastfeeding is a lovely way for you and your baby to get to know each other. But it is not the only way. As babies grow, they become able to form relationships with other people, in other ways: it is the quality of the interaction that creates the bond, not the transfer of nutrients. Fathers keen to bond can relate to their babies by taking part in all the many other ways available – there's no need for anyone to feel excluded.

A crying baby is a hungry baby so you can't be making enough milk.

Babies cry for lots of reasons – they may want a cuddle or some attention, or be bored or tired, or uncomfortable. In fact, crying is usually a late cue that your baby is hungry. It is also the case that some small babies, or those who are not well, may not always cry to be fed. If your baby is growing and seems contented (see pages 82–3) she is getting enough milk.

CHAPTER 3

Formula feeding today

Babies have been fed in different ways for probably as long as we have existed, using various vessels and other means of delivery, and foods other than breast milk, as we'll see on page 38. Today, the only universally accepted infant food for a baby who's not breastfed is infant formula milk, almost always given by bottle. The experience of formula feeding, as well as the obvious practicalities, is different from breastfeeding for both baby and mother. This chapter looks more closely at this, and the impact on you and your baby. You'll also understand how formula feeding has become more pervasive in our culture, despite the fact that most women wish to breastfeed and regret stopping, and despite the research that demonstrates the differences in health outcomes between breast- and formula-fed babies.

A brief look back

Branded baby foods have been sold in Western Europe and North America since the middle of the 19th century. However, mothers who did not breastfeed, or who did not fully breastfeed, usually gave their infants cows' milk rather than buy anything special.

Formula – today a commercially produced infant milk made from cows' milk – was first sold in the USA as reputedly individual, custom-made breast milk substitutes. The doctors who devised formulas charged their patients high fees for their products.

In the UK, non-breastfed babies were fed a home-made mix of boiled and diluted cows' milk with added sugar right up until the 1960s, when commercial, 'modified' formulas took over. National Dried Milk, a product originally commissioned by the Government in 1940, was in use until the mid-1970s.

Formulas were largely unmodified at first; they consisted of dried full-fat or semi-skimmed milk, which had to be reconstituted with water, and with added vitamins A and D. From the 1970s, formula was modified – the protein content was partially broken down to make it easier to digest and the sodium content was lowered.

Why did formula become more popular than ever? Part of the reason was the way breastfeeding became more difficult to do, as

the skills and knowledge about how it worked started to fade. This was at least partly because, from the 1950s onwards, more and more mothers had their babies in hospitals or maternity homes and followed hospital-style routines, separated from their babies. Mothers were taught to feed according to the clock, both in frequency and the length of feeds, and they did what they were told. Babycare leaflets at the time recommended four-hourly feeds, each lasting 20 minutes. This was not based on science at all, but possibly related to observations of how bottlefed babies were likely to feed, and fitting in with an industrialised culture's emphasis on schedules and timing.

Breastfeeding really does not work well if it starts off like this: it rarely meets babies' needs, and the protests expressed by babies were perceived to mean 'not enough milk'. Babies were routinely 'topped up' with formula after breastfeeds, and sometimes bottlefed in hospital nurseries at night.

Bottlefeeding was also seen as more convenient than breastfeeding, and doctors and other health professionals often gave no more than lukewarm support to the idea of breastfeeding. A lack of knowledge made it difficult for them to intervene when the effects of scheduling and timed feeds led to breastfeeding going wrong. At the same time, commercial influences on doctors and hospitals, and on aid agencies in the developing world, played a major role in discouraging women from breastfeeding in all countries from the middle of the 20th century onwards.

This is a worldwide scandal and a public health tragedy. It was only in the 1970s that attention was drawn to the serious health risks

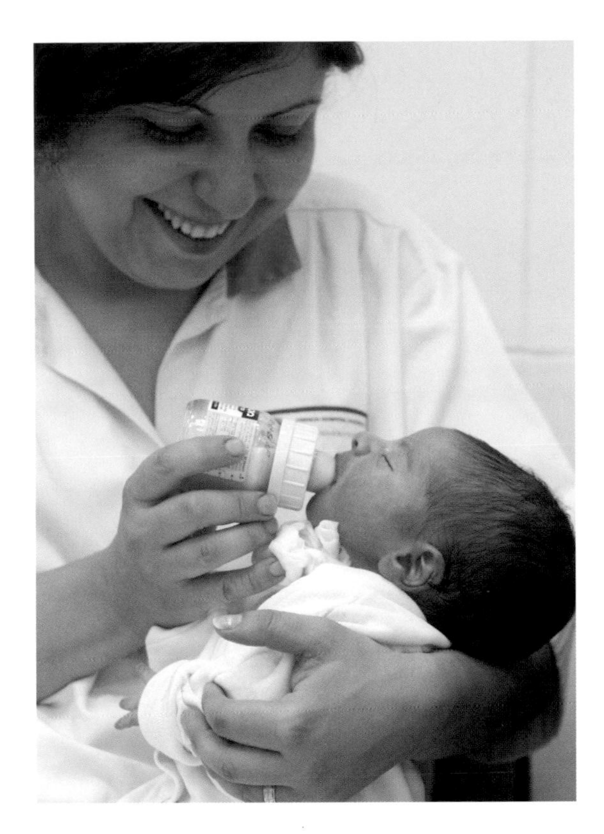

of formula and formula distribution and promotion in the developing world. In 1981, the World Health Organisation drew up the International Code of Marketing of Breastmilk (see feature, pages 46–7), which passed on the message to health workers, governments and agencies that breastfeeding needed careful and vigilant protection.

Today, in most Western countries, the use of formula is widespread and entrenched, but there is confusion among mothers and healthcare professionals about the differences between brands and types. All too often decisions about which type of formula to use are essentially led by marketing, despite the restrictions on advertising in some countries.

What is formula?

Today, some infant milks are called formulas – a throwback to the American doctors who devised so-called individualised formulas in the 19th century (see p. 38). In the UK and about 160 other countries, the composition of formula is subject to the rules laid down by the UN's Food and Agriculture Organisation and the World Health Organisation's international Codex Alimentarius. Governments have to adhere to the Codex rules as a minimum standard.

Every so often, in response to greater nutritional knowledge or changes in industrial processes, the Codex rules are changed. The Codex can be subject to industry lobbying and commercial pressures; for example, manufacturers have successfully prevented costly ingredients being mandatory.

Codex rules make infant formula fairly standard in quality throughout the world. The different formulations are often inspired by marketing as much as nutritional progress, so innovations in one brand are soon matched by similar innovations in another. If you're choosing a brand for your baby, this should actually make life simpler for you, as there are really no huge differences between them, but the packaging does not make this clear. You need to read the package carefully to assess if the product has been formulated for your baby's age. This is not labelled in a uniform way across different brands, and surveys have shown that parents can become confused.

Standard formula available in most Western countries is based on dried and powdered cows' milk, with added vitamins, fatty acids and other substances. The protein content has been modified to make it more digestible and the sodium (salt) content has been reduced.

Some formulas, usually marketed as 'from birth', have a protein content that's higher in whey proteins (easier for a young baby to digest). Other types might be labelled 'for hungrier babies' or 'for older babies', and they are less modified, with protein that's higher in casein, which is tougher and more difficult for a

baby's digestive system to process. This is why such formulas are marketed as being able to keep babies satisfied for longer between feeds. It is legal for these to be sold as suitable from birth, however. The calorie content is the same as whey-dominant formulas.

Other milks

After six months of age, formula-fed babies can have 'follow-on milk', which is casein-dominant and has a higher iron content than standard infant formulas. This product came on to the UK market when legislation preventing formula advertising (defined as products for babies under six months) was introduced. There is no reason why your baby needs follow-on milk; there are no benefits to it compared with standard infant formula, and if your baby seems comfortable and happy, you don't need to switch. Babies do start to need more iron after six months or so, but for most babies this can come from solid foods, which they start at around this time.

More expensive than powdered formula are ready-to-feed versions, which remain in their cartons until being poured into a baby's bottle. For this reason, they are safer than powdered formula, which needs careful preparation to prevent bacterial contamination (see pages 92–3). Current UK and European safety guidelines recommend ready-to-feed formula for sick, pre-term or otherwise vulnerable babies.

Goats' milk formula is available, but it is not currently approved for general use in the UK, as it does not meet the UK Food Standards Agency's criteria. A doctor or paediatric dietitian may recommend it if your baby appears to have a reaction or an intolerance to standard cows' milk formula.

Soya formula – created from soya beans – is approved for use when a baby has been diagnosed with an intolerance or allergy to cows' milk formula. There are concerns about it, however. Soya formula contains plant hormones, known as phytoestrogens, and it's thought these might have a harmful effect, especially on boys' normal development. In addition to its high aluminium content, soya formula also contains a lot of sugar to make it palatable, and this has been associated with several cases of serious tooth decay.

There are other special formulas, intended for non-breastfed babies who can't have any other formula because of health problems, such as congenital lactose intolerance. This condition is very rare. It is caused by an absence of lactase, the enzyme needed to digest lactose. Lactose is the sugar found in all milks, so a lactose-free formula is needed.

Secondary lactose intolerance can develop in a baby who has had a bout of gastroenteritis, and just occasionally, a formula-fed baby might need a lactose-free formula to aid recovery.

Most special formulas are expensive and, in the UK, they can usually be obtained only on prescription. They include rice formula, hypoallergenic formula (in which the protein is broken down already) and elemental formulas, which are synthesised from amino acids.

Bottles

A bottle with a teat on it is generally the easiest and most effective way of giving your baby formula, although a cup, or a cup and spoon, a tube or even a syringe may be used – particularly with premature babies or those born with a cleft palate. For most babies, especially those who are primarily or solely formula fed, a bottle is the method of choice.

A bottle with a teat gives your baby the pleasure and satisfaction of sucking, and while it is not the same action as the sucking involved in breastfeeding, it does use his innate sucking reflexes. Most babies actively enjoy the process of bottlefeeding, in a way that goes beyond getting milk simply to satisfy hunger or thirst.

Feeding vessels fashioned with some sort of spout to enable a sucking motion to remove liquid go back to very early civilisations. Artefacts clearly intended for this purpose have been found in ancient Egyptian, Greek and Roman tombs, for example.

In more recent times, knowledge about the spread of infection through poorly cleaned milk traces led eventually to welcome safety improvements in baby bottles. These drove from the market such products as the so-called murder bottle, a Victorian monstrosity with a long, impossible-to-clean piece of rubber tubing with a teat and valve on the top, inserted into a glass or stone receptacle.

Bottles and teats these days are easy to keep clean. You should discard worn or scratched bottles because it's harder to see if you have cleaned them properly, and because bacteria can lodge inside the scratches.

Modern bottles are made from plastic, and there are rules governing the safety of materials used in their manufacture. (Concerns over bisphenol A as a material led to legislation in the UK and elsewhere banning it, but if you use old bottles passed on from someone else, you can't be sure if they meet today's standards.) Glass bottles are no longer commercially available.

Between uses, all feeding equipment should be sterilised by boiling or with sterilising liquids or tablets dissolved in cold water. Electric or microwave steam sterilisers are probably the quickest and easiest to use (see pages 94–5). Note that in some countries (for instance, the USA) mothers are advised that sterilising bottles in a dishwasher at a high temperature is adequate. There is not a great deal of research to point to this being adequate or not. What is important is to ensure clean, milk-trace-free bottles and teats all the time your baby takes milk from a bottle. The other issue with hygiene and safe preparation is addressed by making up the powder safely with boiled water that is at least 70°C (see page 92).

The emotional experience of formula feeding

Today, in most Western countries, formula feeding is unremarkable. Although it's not the physiological norm, it's socially and culturally 'normal', and most babies in the UK – and the rest of Europe – are fed at least some formula, and a sizeable minority have only formula from birth (UK statistics show that 24 per cent of all babies are formula fed from birth, but there are large social and regional differences).

Yet despite the fact that formula is widely available and bottlefed babies are an everyday sight, there is also widespread acceptance that formula is not as good as breast milk, and that a baby is better nourished on his mother's milk. This belief may also exist alongside a sincere conviction that there's really not much difference between formula and breast milk, that sometimes formula can be better than breast milk, that there's 'too much pressure' put on mothers to breastfeed, and that babies turn out the same way, however they're fed.

I've come across this contradictory stance many times, and this is sensitive territory for anyone writing about, working in or otherwise

MIXED FEEDING

Although the term can be confusing – it used to mean giving solid foods when a baby was still largely breast- or formula fed – mixed feeding now refers to the occasional use of formula as an addition to breastfeeding, for example using formula milk to 'top up' or replace a breastfeed. Its effect on breastfeeding can be to undermine breast milk production and deny a baby the health benefits of exclusive breastfeeding. However, it can be done, and in some situations it's a workable compromise when full breastfeeding is not possible for a particular reason. For example, if breastfeeding has not gone well for you and your baby needs feeding more than you can produce, or if your baby is unable to take what he needs from the breast, you might use formula in addition to breastfeeding. You can find out more about how to use formula feeding in ways that interfere as little as possible with breastfeeding on pages 112–13.

connected to the field of infant feeding. People state that 'You can't tell by looking at children which ones were formula fed and which ones were breastfed', as if that somehow proves it doesn't matter how babies are fed. Or they'll tell you that child A was formula fed and child B was breastfed and child B is more often ill than child A, so that just goes to show…what exactly?

It's difficult to think of something as widespread as formula feeding as being anything other than totally benign. I sometimes hear, 'If there was anything wrong with formula, shops wouldn't be allowed to sell it', which, of course, doesn't follow at all. Babies who are not getting breast milk need formula – it's an essential replacement for human milk. Removing it from sale is not an option, at least not in a country where virtually 100 per cent of babies will require it at some point.

In addition to the presumed suitability of formula, a mother may find it hard to breastfeed for one or more of many physical, social and cultural reasons that are not always within her control. She may also feel the encouragement to breastfeed as pressure and become upset and even feel guilty for not managing to continue to do so. She may resent any suggestion that her baby is not being as well fed as a breastfed baby. That can sound like a suggestion her baby is not as well cared for or even as well loved.

So, it can be difficult for health professionals and other people involved in health promotion or support for new parents to get the 'tone' right. Being honest, and sticking to the facts, about formula, would mean explaining that not breastfeeding does make a difference to mothers and babies. But who wants to sound critical of mothers about such a sensitive topic? There is a natural impulse to protect mothers from guilt and regret about their feeding decisions.

Some researchers speculate that emphasising the health effects of feeding may be the wrong move if we are trying to encourage more breastfeeding. Instead, it's suggested that it's better to focus on the relationship aspects, and explaining how breastfeeding is a means of establishing a close bond between a mother and her baby. The downside to this is that mothers who switch reluctantly to formula may feel just as negative about the idea they are not as close to their babies as their breastfeeding counterparts. We have not got the message, or the medium, right yet.

Infant feeding is a potentially emotional and emotive collection of behaviours, no matter how it's done. Individual mothers read generalised advice, and sit through generalising antenatal class discussions about why breastfeeding is better than formula feeding. If they then don't breastfeed, or if they stop breastfeeding, they hear every word of it as a personal, targeted criticism. We'll see on pages 98–101 how formula feeding does not have to feel hurtful or emotionally distant.

Keep in mind that the vast majority of mothers do the very best they can for their babies. The decisions they make for them are done with their wellbeing in mind, and they should not be judged on their choices. It is a fact that most people don't judge. Most people recognise that nothing in life is as simple as 'breast or bottle?', and that the 'choice' to go for one or the other, or a combination, depends on many factors, some of them personal to the individual mother herself.

FORMULA MARKETING:
RULES, RESTRICTIONS, CODES AND LAWS

The choice to breastfeed needs protection and nurturing in today's world. Marketing and advertising of formula can create pressure on mothers to use formula rather than breastfeed. In addition, the choice to use a particular formula can be influenced by brand promotion, rather than a discussion of how to match the nutritional and health needs of an individual baby. In 1981, these factors were recognised by the World Health Organisation, responding to widespread concern about the way formula manufacturers of all types, in all parts of the world, were using marketing techniques both to undermine breastfeeding, and to actively promote formula brands to the public and to healthcare professionals.

The result was the WHO International Code of Marketing of Breastmilk Substitutes, now known as the WHO/UNICEF Code, which was adopted by the World Health Assembly. It's been added to and enhanced and clarified since then. It is intended for all countries, developing and developed, and covers all foods, drinks and bottles and teats which babies might have instead of breast milk. It does not restrict their availability, but

Key points of the Code include a ban on

- promotion to the general public, including free samples or special offers
- marketing to healthcare professionals that has no scientific or factual basis
- idealised pictures on the packaging of formula (pictures of chubby babies, for instance)
- false or misleading health claims (including catchlines like 'closest to breast milk' or 'best for your baby's immune system'

Packs must include clear instructions on safe preparation in the local language.

it does set out ways they should be marketed ethically.

In the UK, Baby Milk Action, a member of IBFAN (International Baby Food Action Network, page 144, monitors adherence to the Code.

The WHO Code is not law in any Western country, but most have some sort of marketing restriction on infant formula. In the UK, for instance, formula intended for babies under six months old is subject to some marketing restrictions. Nonetheless the law is weaker than the WHO Code in scope and routinely flouted.

UK mothers see invitations online and in leaflets and magazines to join a formula manufacturer's 'baby club', which brings with it free gifts (a soft toy, a garment for the baby). Telephone helplines give advice on anything to do with babycare, not just feeding.

Of course, very few women would change their chosen way of feeding just because they'd received a branded teddy bear in the post. But, overall, these tactics work on affirming the brand and affirming formula feeding – a baby wearing a branded bib or playing with a branded cuddly toy is a live advertisement for the product. All manufacturers know that feeling good about a product is an important marketing tool: some mothers may actively choose brand X if they have had a free gift and a warm chat with a telephone adviser; other mothers may respond to the endorsement of product named on a bib as an implied recommendation by a friend.

CHAPTER 4

Getting started with breastfeeding

If your baby is born healthy and at term (37 weeks' gestation onwards), she is well equipped with reflexes and, crucially, the desire to stay close to you and to breastfeed for food, drink and comfort. The early days are not always easy. Sometimes, events connected with labour and birth or confusion about your baby's needs and behaviour, can get in the way of a good start, which is unfortunate, as breastfeeding that starts well is likely to continue for longer.

It's good to have some understanding of how breastfeeding actually works, and to be able to share this with other people who may misinterpret normal breastfeeding as problematic and whose offers of help – though well-meaning – might be undermining. It's also important to know how to check that things are going well in the first days and weeks; if you are able to spot the early signs of something not being quite right, you'll be better able to nip any problems in the bud.

How breastfeeding works

Virtually every mother produces breast milk simply as a result of being pregnant and going through labour.

In pregnancy

You are likely to feel and see some differences in your breasts during pregnancy – sometimes right from the start – because hormonal changes cause you to start making tissue that will produce and store breast milk. In addition, small spots on your nipples and areolae may become more prominent. Known as Montgomery's tubercles, these are the visible portion of small sebaceous glands in the nipples and areolae. These glands secrete an oily fluid, which helps prevent the skin from drying out, and prepare the nipples and areolae for breastfeeding.

About halfway through pregnancy, colostrum starts to be made: this process is termed lactogenesis 1. Higher in protein and lower in fat that breast milk, colostrum will satisfy your baby's needs in the first few days. In the last few weeks of pregnancy, you may be aware of slight leaking which might dry as a sort of crust on your nipples or make the inside of your bra damp. On the other hand, you may not notice anything at all. Nonetheless colostrum production is certainly happening.

HOW BREASTS MAKE MILK

Breast milk is made by the alveoli: minuscule sacs made up of cells that extract water, lactose, amino acids, minerals, vitamins and many other necessary ingredients from your blood and fat stores.

At first, milk production is all hormonally driven, and happens whether or not you ever put your baby to the breast. In the first few days after birth, your baby's suckling (or your expressing milk) supports the formation of prolactin receptor sites within the alveoli. These sites attract prolactin, which circulates in your bloodstream, in order to stimulate milk production. Early and frequent feeding sets up more prolactin receptors, which enable effective milk production for as long as you breastfeed. This is a good reason not to restrict your baby's access to the breast.

After the first days, milk produced by hormones acting on the breast (known as endocrine production) is superseded by that which comes from within the breast itself (known as autocrine production). As milk is removed, the breasts learn how much more they need to make and how quickly they need to make it. When the alveoli are full of milk, the prolactin receptors become distorted so that prolactin cannot enter the alveoli and milk production is slowed down. When the alveoli are emptied of their milk, the prolactin receptors regain their previous shape, start attracting prolactin again and milk production increases.

In addition, breast milk contains a small protein which researchers have named 'feedback inhibitor of lactation', or FIL. This works on the alveoli's milk-making cells to slow down production so that the more milk that remains in the breast, the more FIL is present, and the greater the slow-down effect. The opposite is true, as well: when there is less milk in the breast, there is less FIL, and milk is made faster. Because of this, milk production is largely driven by your baby; the more she feeds, the more milk you make. If your baby is unable to feed effectively (perhaps because she is sick or pre-term or breastfeeding has not got off to a good start), you can express milk to set up production in this 'use it or lose it' fashion.

THE STRUCTURE OF THE BREAST

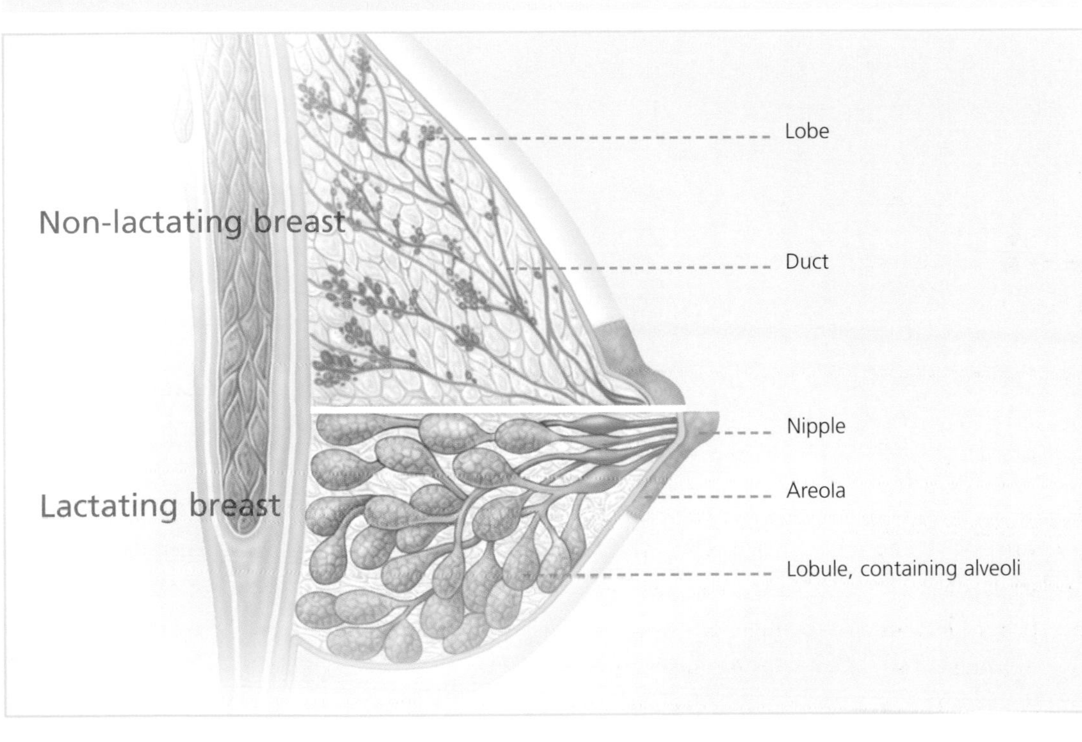

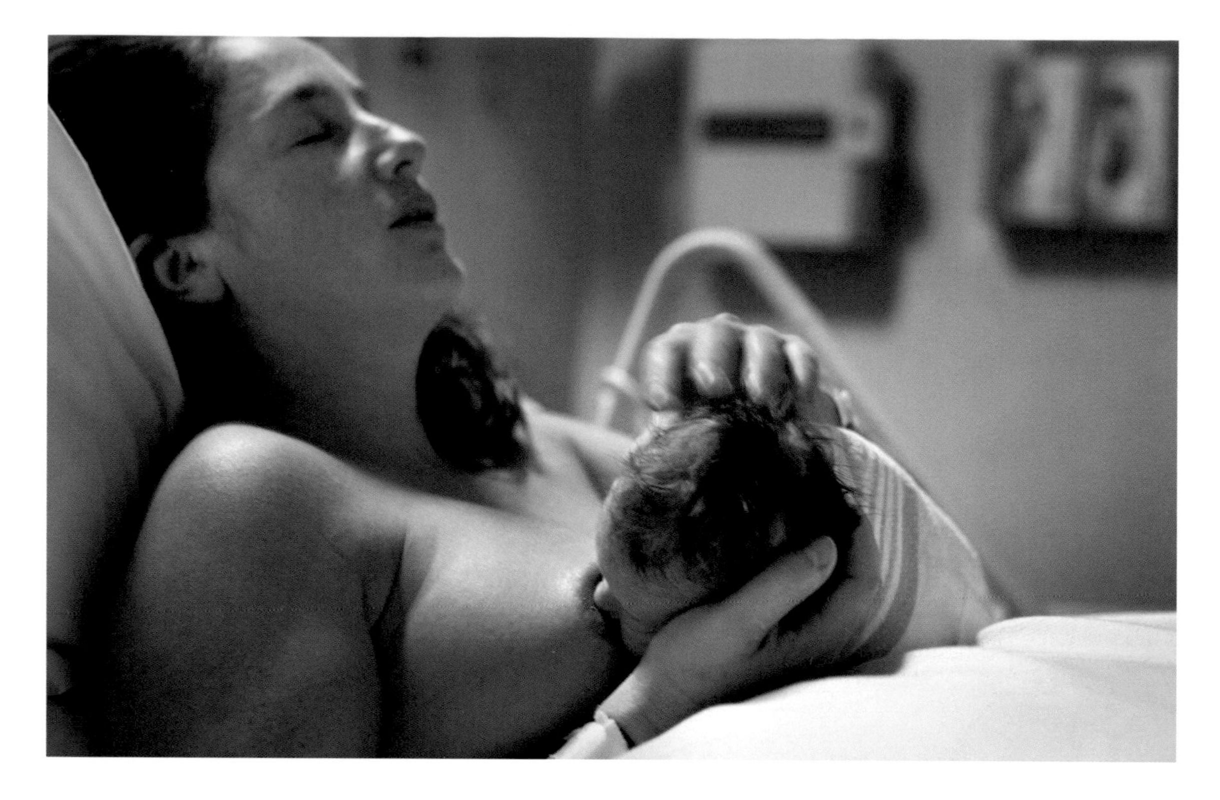

During the birth and immediately after

During the third stage of labour, when the placenta comes away from the uterine wall, your body starts producing milk under the stimulation of the hormone prolactin. If your baby is put to your breast straight away (see page 56), colostrum will be there for her. (The placenta secretes progesterone, which inhibits the action of prolactin, thereby curbing its milk-making effects until the placenta is shed.)

After the first days

As the days go by after the birth, more mature milk takes the place of colostrum. This milk appears in greater volume, so you may notice your breasts become much larger, although some women see and feel either no changes or only small ones. This process is known as your milk 'coming in' (technically, lactogenesis 2) and it generally happens any time from day 2 to as late as day 6 or 7, though most women notice it on day 3. Some effectively feeding babies cope very easily with the extra milk and start taking it in as soon as it appears for them.

It's from this point onwards that milk starts to be made in response to its removal from the breasts – and it's this removal that drives the milk supply. The more often milk is removed, the more milk you'll make. This is why you can make enough for a big baby or a small baby, for a new baby or an older baby, or for twins or triplets.

Neither a clock, timetable nor any sort of schedule can help you or your body in any way. Indeed, anyone who tells you that babies need to feed no more often than every so many hours or for no longer than so many minutes doesn't understand effective breastfeeding. Your body will respond to your baby and not to a clock or someone else's memory of what her baby was like. (You can read more about this response effect and the way your baby creates her own milk supply – as long as her cues are responded to – on page 82.)

Meeting your baby's needs

In the 1980s and '90s, research into how breastfeeding actually worked revealed that breast milk is not uniform – principally, the fat content is changeable and it changes according to the volume of milk in the breast. When the breast is fuller, there is more water and when emptier, more fat.

While this research told us more about breastfeeding and breast milk, it also created problems. Healthcare workers, breastfeeding supporters, writers of babycare books and mothers themselves started to worry whether a baby was receiving the creamier, more calorific hind milk, or whether she was getting too much of the thinner and more watery fore milk. Concepts such as the 'fore milk–hind milk imbalance' arose and pressure grew to ensure that babies were on the breast long enough to somehow battle through the fore milk at the start of the feed in order to get to the more valuable calories in the hind milk.

The reality, however, is that the breasts make only one milk (colostrum, see page 50, is an earlier form), which is stored in the alveoli. Because its creamier components are stickier, this part of the milk is let down (see page 54) somewhat less readily, so the milk the baby gets when the breasts are fuller is higher in water content. When the breasts are emptier the remaining milk is creamier.

The amount of fat in the milk is commensurate with the volume of milk in the breast at the time. In other words, a baby on a

UNDER-DEVELOPED REFLEXES

If your baby was born pre-term (less than or equal to 36 weeks' gestation), her sucking, swallowing and breathing reflexes may not be immediately obvious. This does not mean your pre-term baby cannot be helped and encouraged to breastfeed, but she may need to be given expressed breast milk or formula indirectly (normally via a tube so that she doesn't need to suck), either all or some of the time until she is a bit more developed.

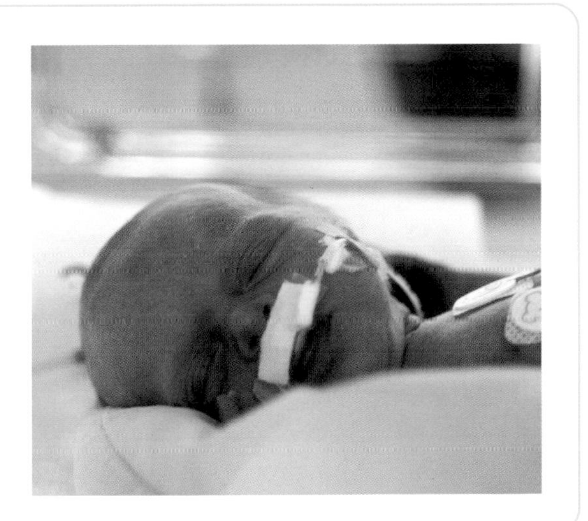

breast that is relatively full will get a higher volume of lower calorie milk, while one on a relatively empty breast will get a lower volume of higher calorie milk. All this is fine, and it's part of the natural, responsive way breastfeeding works as a partnership between mother and baby.

After a while, research shows that generally the milk becomes somewhat higher in fat, as the actual volume of milk made tends to decrease. After a year or so, it becomes higher in protein. These changes are quite small, but are in line with what we know about babies' growth and developmental needs.

Feeding your baby when she seems to ask and letting her suck for as long as she wants allows your body to calibrate your supply to meet her needs. When your breasts are empty, you make milk quickly; when your breasts remain full, your production slows down. Leaving breasts full for too long, however, will interfere with your milk production (and subsequently things can go wrong – see pages 78–9 and 82–3).

The let-down reflex

Milk is made and stored in the alveoli of the breast; when a baby starts to suckle, the hormone oxytocin is stimulated and this works on tiny muscles surrounding the alveoli, which then manage to push the milk out and down the ducts towards the nipple – and from there into a baby's mouth. This release of milk is called the 'let-down' or 'milk-ejection' reflex.

In the first few days after birth, oxytocin is released whenever your baby suckles. As time passes, merely thinking about your baby (or seeing or hearing a baby) can trigger the hormone's release and some women find that their breasts leak when this happens. You can stop this from happening by pressing the heel of your hand into your breast. Some mothers let down on both breasts when feeding, and need to do the 'heel of hand' trick when the baby is on one side, to stop the other breast from reacting, too. This sort of sensitivity tends to get better after a few weeks.

You may experience the let-down reflex as a tingling or a little discomfort, even occasionally as pain. Once breastfeeding is established, however, you are likely to notice it less and less.

Born to breastfeed

Your baby came into the world with the necessary skills and desires to sustain her own physical survival, and more than that, to engage with you to ensure her emotional wellbeing and growing understanding.

At birth, she exhibited reflexes (some of which were assessed or observed as part of a new baby health check, because their presence is a useful confirmation that a newborn is healthy), which enabled her to feed. They include:

- The rooting reflex, which your baby uses to search for your breast, turning her head from side to side, and bobbing around for the right spot to start latching on.
- Sucking and swallowing reflexes evoked by the sensation of your breast and nipple tissue in her mouth enable her to start to remove and swallow milk.
- The stepping reflex, which enables your baby to crawl up to your breast from your abdomen (although it is only one of many ways your baby can come to the breast).

Breastfeeding and attachment

You are more likely to meet your baby's emotional needs when breastfeeding because you are able to react more quickly to her feeding cues. Offering the breast is easier than preparing a bottle, so your baby has less time to become distressed and, if she does become upset, she can be comforted more quickly. The lack of stress means that levels cortisol (see box, page 13) remain normal, and the positive experience of being breastfed lays down strong mental and emotional foundations.

Breastfeeding supports good attachment and warm, loving relationships between mothers and babies for several reasons:

- Mother and baby are physically close, making skin-to-skin contact easy to achieve.
- Feeding takes place frequently throughout the day and night, which creates many opportunities for interaction.
- Only the mother actually does it, which suits the nature of a baby's early social relationships as largely 'dyadic' (made up of two people).
- Baby and mother work as a partnership – the baby 'orders' her milk and the mother creates the supply.
- It is reciprocal; it takes two people, acting cooperatively and giving each other signals. A mother will benefit from a positive affect on her mood, outlook and relationship with her baby, if it proceeds well.
- The baby can use the breast for comfort or non-nutritive sucking, an important way of staying in touch with her mother.

There is no evidence that breastfeeding alone causes or ensures a secure attachment, but research shows a strong link. In one study, mothers who chose to breastfeed showed greater sensitivity to their babies at the age of three months than did bottlefeeding mothers. This could, however, prove that mothers who are already sensitive to their babies' needs are more likely to breastfeed.

Feeding cues

Your baby may show a range of feeding cues designed to prompt you to put her to your breast (or offer a bottle). Young babies are usually ready to feed when:

- they make mouth movements
- they wave their hands
- they kick their legs
- they suck their fingers or hands
- they start to fuss
- they turn their heads as if looking for the breast.

None of these mean your baby must feed this very moment and, sometimes, they are indications your baby needs a cuddle, some interaction with you, or the chance to snuggle to sleep. It can be confusing, and you will not always get your response right. But it's always fine to at least offer a feed, and to accept that these cues can happen, even after you think she's had 'enough'.

FIRST AND LATER FEEDS

Ideally, your baby will begin breastfeeding well from birth, though each day is a little different. You and your newborn will be close most of the day and night, and will enjoy several occasions when you watch each other's face, gaze into each other's eyes, and have little conversations together. You should watch for your baby's feeding cues (see page 55) and because you are close, it should be easy for you to make your breasts available to her.

There will be a few difficult starts, when your baby won't seem sure that she's comfortable, and a few times when you are certain your baby wants to feed but after a couple of sucks, she falls into a deep sleep, but most feeds will start well and not end as clearly as this.

Sometimes, particularly as your baby gets older, you will find that she is feeding in 'clusters', with no marked beginning and end; she will seem to enjoy and need feeding little and often, for a period of a few hours. Many mums report this happening in the evenings, but it can happen at any time. Sometimes, these so-called cluster feeds end with a long, contented sleep.

As we've seen, some of your baby's feeding behaviour is reflexive (see page 54) but much is social and demonstrates your baby's ability to react to the world around her and to you. From birth, she has the ability to focus on objects 20–25 cm away from her own eyes – about the distance between her face and yours when she comes to the breast. She also

This is a typical starting point for many babies about to feed and shows the baby just before she tips her head back...

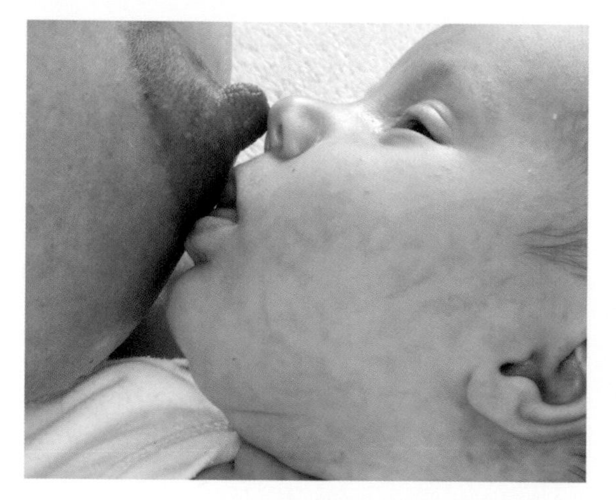

...ready to use her tongue to draw the nipple into the top part of her mouth. Her chin has come close into the breast and her nose is free.

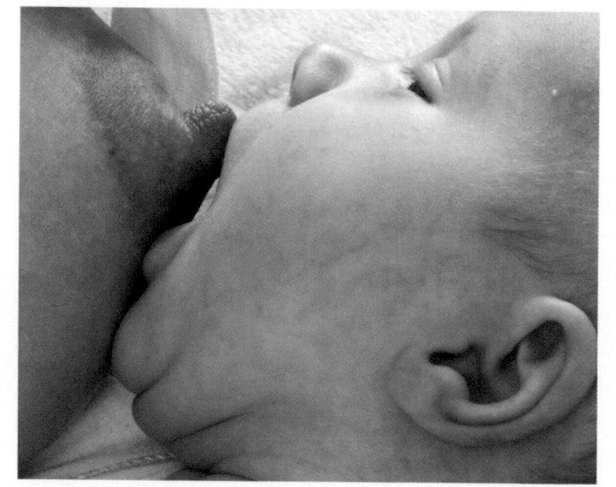

will be affected by your smell, your taste, the touch of your skin and the sound of your voice (when inside you, she could hear you and this familiarity helps her feel at home and relaxed with you). She will calm and settle when she is close to you; she wants to be with you.

Latching on

The only rules about positioning and attaching your baby – often called 'latching on' – are that you should both be comfortable and that your baby should have an effective feed – one that meets her needs for comfort and nutrition.

You may have been taught or read about a particular way to position your baby and yourself, a way to sit, to place your hands and arms, and where and how your baby should lie.

However, you will not have a comfortable, effective feed unless your baby has a good mouthful of breast tissue, and is able to use her tongue and jaw to remove the milk. This usually means that the nipple heads towards the top of the mouth, over the tongue, and towards the back of the mouth, with the dome of your baby's palate fully 'occupied' by your breast.

If your breast is not far enough into her mouth, she is likely to compress your nipple with her tongue, against the roof of her mouth – and that can hurt. A lot. It can damage the nipple to such an extent that the skin breaks, but it can still be very painful even if there is nothing to see (see page 81).

Most babies find it easier to do all of this if they are close in to the mother's body, and if they don't have to turn their heads over their shoulders. However, older babies especially manage to breastfeed perfectly happily in some odd-looking postures, so if it is working for you, and your baby is happy, healthy and growing, this is not something you need to feel you must change.

She has come closer with a good mouthful of breast, and is in a position to get an effective feed, by milking the breast with her tongue and lower jaw.

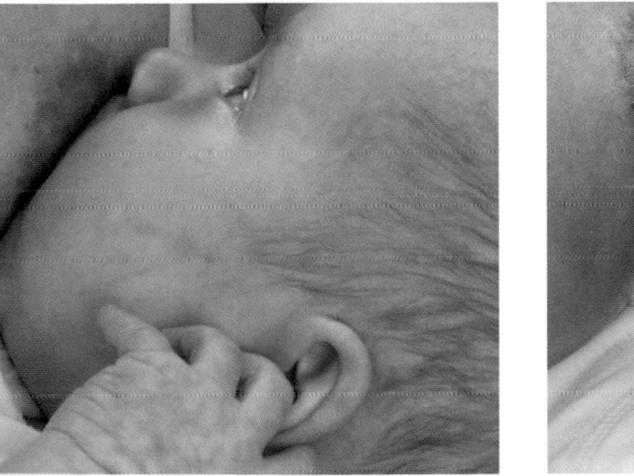

At the end of the feed, she drops off the breast. If your nipple shape is undistorted and she seems contented, chances are it's going well.

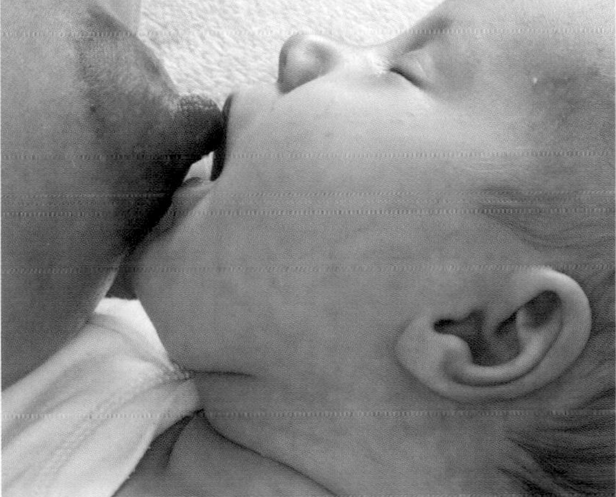

Holding your baby

As long as you and your baby are comfortable, and your baby manages to get your milk effectively, it really doesn't matter how you're positioned together.

You'll find your own ways to feed comfortably and happily. There may be a couple of favourite places in your house where it's light and calm, and you can have everything you need close at hand (see page 65).

Easy-access clothing is essential. Wear a bra that supports your breasts with cups that open separately and wide straps that won't dig in to your shoulders. Day and night your clothing should be easy to lift up or have a front opening. For advice on clothing when out and about see pages 86–7.

At first the birth itself may affect the position you adopt. A mother who has had an episiotomy may be more comfortable lying down than sitting, while a caesarean may mean her wound is too tender for her baby to lie across. In this case, the rugby hold with the baby's feet tucked under her arm may be more comfortable (see below) or try lying side-by-side.

Rugby hold

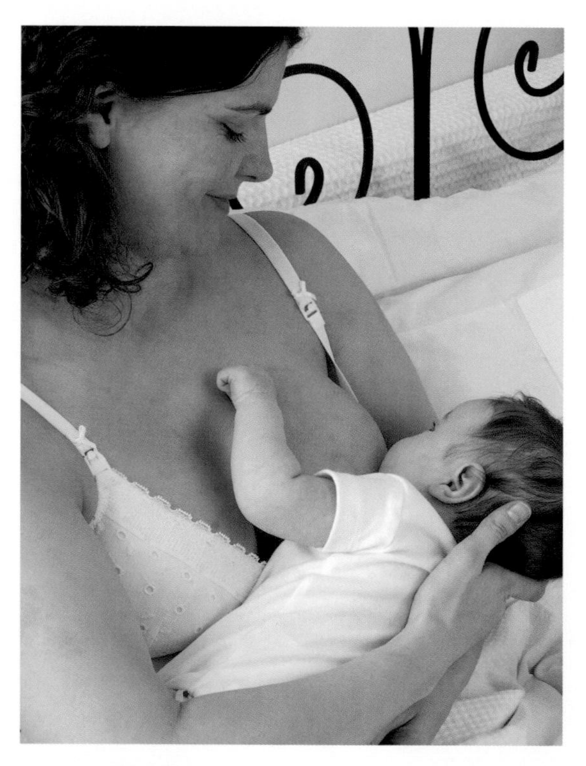

Cross-cradle hold

Check out the choice

- lying side-by-side
- lying side-by-side, baby on mother's upper breast
- lying side-by-side, baby on mother's lower breast
- biological nurturing positions – mother reclined, semi-reclined, in bath, on sofa or chair, in bed
- mother sitting upright, with the baby across the mother's body, her hand towards the baby's feet or behind her shoulder
- baby in a rugby or 'underarm' hold

Recent research indicates the value of feeding positions that differ from the ones we tend to see a lot – where a baby lies on her back or side. Researchers refer to a 'biological nurturing' position in which a baby lies lengthwise on her mother's abdomen. If a mother reclines or semi-reclines, this enables a 'lengthwise baby' to self-attach. The mother's hand and body movements seem to work in instinctive harmony, holding, stroking, cradling or otherwise helping her baby when she needs it.

For advice on your comfort while you breastfeed, see page 65.

Lying side-by-side

Twins

Special 'V'-shaped feeding pillows are available, which support each baby's head and shoulders leaving your hands and forearms free, if you need them.

Breastfeeding twins

If both your twins are well, feed them as soon as you can after the birth. If feeding straight away isn't possible – perhaps because one or both of the babies needs some extra care – then you may need to express milk for them as soon as you can (see page 106).

Most mothers of twins have no fixed pattern for feeding both babies at once or not: sometimes, one way just seems easier than the other. Some mothers breastfeed both babies and others breastfeed one and give expressed milk to the other, either rotating between the two babies or always giving one expressed milk. Either way will ensure you have sufficient milk but you may need to keep a record of which twin you've been feeding in which way. Because new babies need to feed frequently at first, feeding separately can mean almost literally all-day-and-all-night feeding/changing/settling. Doing it two at a time can make things a little easier.

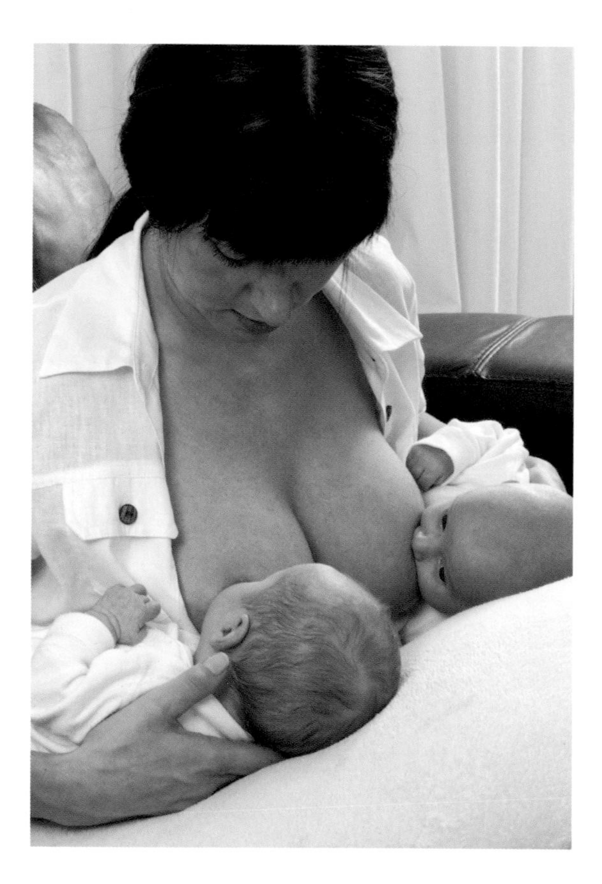

An early drawback to breastfeeding both twins at once, however, is that you have no 'spare hand' at the time when your babies are still learning to latch on and stay on. This may mean you feel uncomfortably 'trapped'; you won't be able to scratch your nose, move your hair or sip a drink. If one baby loses her latch, it can be hard to get her back on again. A 'V'-shaped pillow can help (see page 59). Even if both twins latch on successfully right away, you really will need another pair of hands at first.

Encouraging your babies to have the same timetable isn't going to work all the time – there will be moments when one twin is fast asleep and resists waking for feeding, while the other shows she really won't wait another minute. It's worth bathing your babies together, and at least offering a feed to both when one seems to want one, in order to work towards some degree of predictability into your days.

In the 'football' hold, each baby is positioned under one of your arms with her legs tucked behind your back.

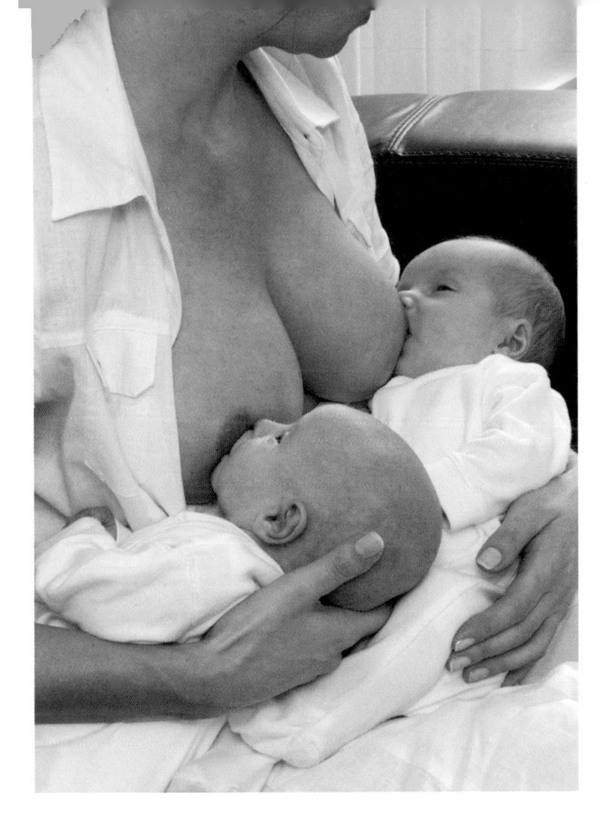

In the parallel hold, both babies are held against your chest with their heads facing in the same direction.

One breast per baby?

You can keep each baby at the same breast if you wish, but it's not necessary, In fact, many twin babies eventually develop a preference for one breast over the other, so if you don't want this to happen, it is better to alternate the babies at each feed during the early weeks. Bear in mind, however, that many twins have unequal 'skills' at breastfeeding, at least at first, so making sure each breast gets the stimulation of the 'better' feeder is also a good idea while you are establishing your milk supply. Creating a routine is easier when both babies are of a similar size and have similar feeding patterns. It can take time to establish a routine – probably at least six weeks – but once you have one, it will be much easier.

Keeping a written record at first may be helpful and some women use coloured ribbons pinned to their bras as reminders of which baby fed at which breast last time around.

It's fine to swap and to offer the other breast to each baby, but you will almost certainly find your supply is all right without doing that. In fact, most mothers of twins build up a very good milk supply, as long as the babies are fed frequently, which orders the milk to be made in sufficient quantities for two. Feeding twins provides double the stimulus to the breasts as a singleton and therefore if one twin is a poor feeder or becomes ill, the breasts continue to be stimulated by the other. (Breastfeeding can be easier with two infants than bottlefeeding – you have nothing to buy, nothing to wash, sterilise or store and nothing to prepare.)

Different positions

Feeding two at a time can be done in a number of ways – though the time to experiment is not when either of your babies is eager to be fed or when they're sleepy. You may find that a position that didn't work when your twins were new becomes easier when they're older. If getting positioned with both at once is more than you can manage at first, ask someone to cuddle one baby while you feed the other.

The most popular positions include the 'football' and parallel holds. Another common position with young infants is to hold your babies in a 'V' shape with their feet either touching or crossed over each other. Or, you can hold one baby in the football hold and the other across your lap. Whatever position you choose, you're likely to need some support – either for your back or to raise your babies to the breast.

A mother's nutritional needs

Mothers are often told, or they read in books and other literature, or simply know because it's common sense, that they need to pay attention to their own diet while they are breastfeeding. It is thought, even assumed, that the quality and quantity of breast milk are affected by what you eat. Moreover, if you're having a problem with supply, or your baby seems unsettled or if her growth is faltering, then eating more or better quality, or even different types of food, may be one of the first things suggested if you ask for advice. The facts are clear, however.

Your diet, quality or quantity or type, has a virtually negligible effect on your breastfeeding. For the majority of mothers and babies, it really does not matter what you eat, when or how much – at least not in terms of the breastfeeding experience. You may feel better yourself if you make changes in how you eat, and if you drink enough water to stay hydrated, and your general health long term may benefit, but as regards your breastfeeding, your diet makes no difference.

This has been shown many times in various research projects – babies gain weight and thrive just fine, even when mothers are on poor diets or their food intake is very restricted. Give mothers more food, and it makes no difference to their babies. Pure observation shows the same results – it's noted that in war zones, prison camps and sieges and so on where food is in short supply, that if mothers continue to breastfeed, their babies continue to flourish. The babies' growth normally only starts to falter if breastfeeding is interrupted in some way, or when with older babies, breastfeeding ceases or becomes intermittent, and sufficient solid foods are not available.

These truths are counter-intuitive as we assume that the body needs to be in tip-top nutritional health to make breastfeeding a success. But nature sees it differently.

For most of human history, food has not been in plentiful supply. Our bodies evolved to cope with periods of food shortage. Human in the 21st century certainly tend to eat far more than they need, on the whole. During pregnancy, a woman's body lays down spare fat to provide the energy to make milk after the birth. A woman's metabolism changes in pregnancy and while breastfeeding so she gets maximum value out of the calories/energy she takes in. That means that although a mother may provide (say) a litre of milk for her infant a day – which equates to an energy value of something like 700 calories – she does not need to eat or drink 700 calories in order to make it. Really, she doesn't.

It's normal to feel a little hungrier than usual when breastfeeding. To feel comfortable, refreshed and energised, it makes sense to eat when you feel you want to. The oft-repeated advantage of breastfeeding that it helps you lose weight may or may not be true for every individual, but generally speaking, if you feel like snacking, or having a second helping, go ahead. But don't expect it to help your milk production.

Breast milk is, however, linked with your diet in other ways. Your milk can acquire

different flavours related to your diet. This is thought to be a good thing – milk is subtly preparing the baby for the changes that will come as she moves on to family foods. Occasionally, mothers report their baby seems to object to breastfeeding and link it with a particular food eaten in the previous few hours. It is difficult to know, however, if this is really a flavour the baby doesn't like.

Essential nutrients

If you have a normal diet, there's not a great deal you can do to actually change the composition of your breast milk. However, if you are chronically short of some nutrients (vitamin D, iron, some fatty acids) and have poor stores, your breast milk may be unable to source them in sufficient quantities. That said, there's not much evidence that this has significant detrimental effects on the growth of your baby. She will grow just fine – we're talking about the precise levels of particular nutrients in breast milk here, rather than the capacity of breast milk to ensure normal, healthy growth. There seems to be no evidence at all – and it has been looked for – that breastfed babies of poorly nourished mothers suffer in any measurable way, as long as solid foods are introduced at an appropriate time.

This is particularly the case with iron, as mothers who are short of iron may have babies who were born with less iron 'in store' and who will need solids which contain iron when they move on from breast milk only.

A possible exception is vitamin D: there are good arguments for giving drops, especially to older breastfed babies (in the UK supplements are already added to formula). Mothers should take a look at their own lifestyles and diets to improve their own levels, particularly if they live in northern climates and are from darker-skinned ethnic groups. We spend far more time inside than our ancestors ever did, and breast milk evolved when we routinely had more sunlight on our skin (the body makes vitamin D from sunlight).

Vegan mothers should probably take vitamin B12 supplements to ensure its presence in breast milk and protect the baby from a range of developmental disorders associated with deficiency in this vitamin. (Vitamin B12 is only found in animal products.)

For information about allergies and intolerances in babies and their relation to early feeding, see page 129.

YOUR OWN COMFORT

Your own comfort while you feed your baby is important when you are breastfeeding – in the beginning at least you are likely to spend a lot of time feeding – and this is even more important if you have had a caesarean.

Night feeds are usually easier if you take your baby into bed with you (if you are not co-sleeping already, see pages 118–19) and a lot of mothers lie on the bed to feed by day at least some of the time too. Otherwise, choose a comfortable supportive chair or sofa that allows you to sit with both feet on the floor or a footstool. Support your back and arms with cushions and have a 'spare' so that you can shift position easily and still support your back. You may want a cushion in your lap to raise your baby closer too. You shouldn't need to lean forward, as this will put unnecessary strain on your back and shoulders and soon cause backache. If there's a table where you can put all the other bits and pieces that make it easier to concentrate on feeding your baby without interruption, so much the better. Otherwise put whatever you can in a basket or on a tray.

Getting it all together

These are the things you might want to have to hand when you settle down to feed your baby.

- A couple of cushions
- TV or radio remote
- Bottle of water or juice and/or a snack
- Book or magazines
- Phone
- Muslins or dribble cloths

If you have another child who is going to need your attention too, be sure you also have a snack or drink for him and a couple of things for him to do: if the baby's feed takes a long time, a single book probably won't keep him happy!

Breastfeeding aids

Normally, you don't need to do anything special to keep your breasts and nipples comfortable and working as they should. After all, breastfeeding evolved long before anyone developed any products or garments to support it. However, there are a number of items you can use that might be helpful, depending on your circumstances and experience.

Nursing bras

There are several styles available to enable you to let your baby have access to your breasts, one at a time – a drop cup arrangement, a lift the flap design, or a zip opening at the front. Most styles are supportive, because that's more comfortable for most women, especially in the early days when your breasts are likely to be larger than usual. Look for styles that have adjustable shoulder straps and fastenings at the back that allow you to adjust the circumference of the bra, to cope with fluctuating breast size.

Nipple shields

These are rubber or silicone coverings that go over your nipples. They're sometimes used as a protector if nipples are damaged, or as a way of offering the baby assistance in getting well latched. While they are sometimes useful as a tool, they have drawbacks. For instance, they can fall off or slip just as you're getting the baby on or when she relaxes her sucking. They don't really teach the baby to take a good mouthful of breast milk, and the baby is no better at this when the shield is removed. In addition, babies can become very keen on the shield and resist the unfamiliarity of the breast. There's also some research that shows babies have difficulty removing sufficient milk with the shield in place, and after a while, this can reduce supply.

If a shield is suggested to you, don't feel you have to avoid it, but ask your midwife or health visitor or whoever is assessing you about tackling the problems which led to needing a shield, so these can be resolved.

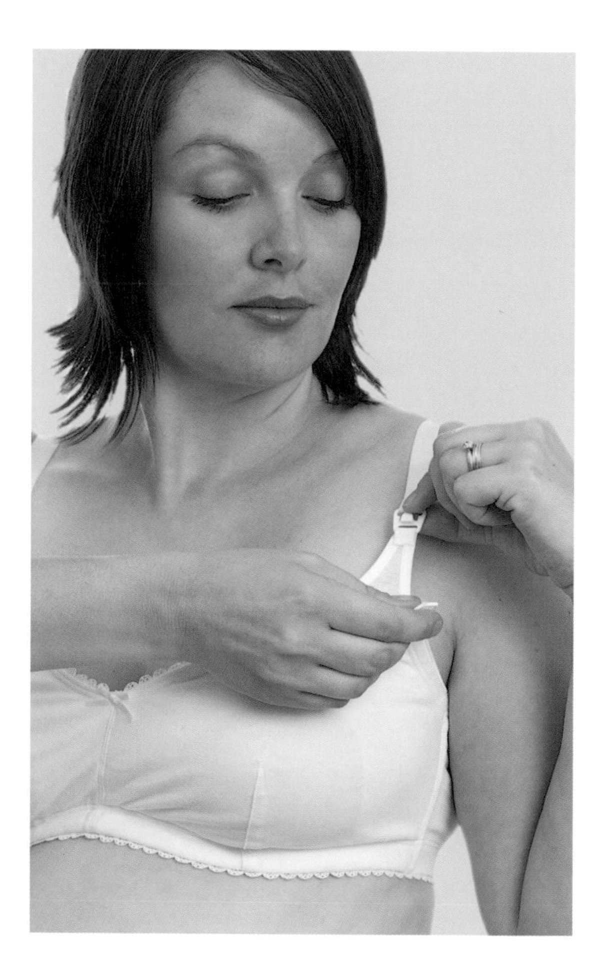

Breast pads

Some women leak breast milk, though this doesn't go on for long (most women find it stops after a couple of months or so). You can put pads – disposables, washable fabric ones, or ones made of silicone that adhere to your skin – into your bra cups to protect your clothing. Alternatively, use folded cotton handkerchiefs, and wash them.

Breast shells

These are plastic covers in two parts that click together, which catch leaked milk, and which were originally designed to make flat or inverted nipples stand out. The study that looked at their efficacy for this found they made no difference.

Nipple everters

There is anecdotal evidence that some individual mothers have found that nipple everters are effective at drawing out inverted nipples, but there has been no comparative study into their use.

Other accessories

These include warming pads of sheepskin or wool, which are especially popular in Scandinavia; nipple creams, which may soothe damaged skin but that should never be used without careful attention to helping your baby take the breast in a way that doesn't hurt you; cooling pads to relieve engorgement (see pages 80–1); and breastfeeding cushions – available in several different styles and shapes – aimed at supporting and holding your baby more easily.

Breast pumps – manual or electrical – can be very useful as an easy way to express milk for your baby. See pages 106–7 for more on expressing breast milk.

Individual women may find some products helpful but none of them is essential. In particular, some cushions may actually make it more difficult for a baby at the breast to get a really close and effective attachment. Mothers with back problems or a disability may find a pillow or cushion helpful, and mothers who have had a caesarean section sometimes appreciate a cushion to avoid pressure on the scar in the early days. Speak to other mothers, and try before you buy if you can.

CHAPTER 5

Challenges and concerns in breastfeeding

Not everything goes smoothly with breastfeeding – even when it goes well at the start, you might hit unexpected pitfalls later on. Or you may have the biggest challenges at the beginning if your baby is born pre-term, or is otherwise vulnerable.

Worrying about whether or not your baby's intake of milk is sufficient is quite common in a world which likes to measure, assess and compare; and some mothers find breastfeeding uncomfortable and even painful.

It's not possible – and it would be unfair – to say 'everything' that challenges happy breastfeeding can be overcome with the right circumstances, treatment, support and information.

Women who switch to formula feeding, or who supplement with formula, in the face of breastfeeding problems sometimes get very irritated when it's suggested that if only they had done x, y or z, everything would have been just fine. But there's a lot you can do to fix things, or even to avoid the worst effects of problems, or to spot a possible problem on the horizon and take measures to make it less of an issue.

Birth concerns

Breastfeeding gets off to the easiest, most comfortable start when a baby is born alert and healthy. The first hour or two after birth is a time when your baby's likely to be awake and responsive and ready to find the breast. He may be able to attach with a little help and guidance from you and enjoy a first feed. However, the birth itself may have an effect on your baby's early feeding.

Pain relief

A baby's innate desire to feed may be affected by the drugs used to relieve your pain during labour and delivery. Talk about your choice of pain relief with a midwife in advance so you'll know what your options are when the time comes. Pethidine and other opiates (like diamorphine) cross the placenta and affect a baby's breathing, sucking reflex and general alertness, sometimes for a couple of days or more (the longer before the birth the drugs are given, the lesser the effects on your baby).

Studies on the effects of epidurals on a baby's behaviour are inconclusive, but some experts believe that the drug used in the injection may make a difference. Epidurals may increase the incidence of birth interventions, like forceps or ventouse, and it could be that the after-effects of assisted delivery – rather than the epidural itself – cause a baby to feed less well, perhaps because of a bit of a headache.

On the other hand, 'gas and air' (entonox) is quickly expelled from your body and will not affect the baby.

Other forms of pain relief like relaxation, controlled breathing or distraction techniques, won't have any effect on your baby's responses, but they may not be strong enough.

If you have a choice of pain relief, bear these issues in mind and be aware that a baby affected by pain relief might need extra opportunities and extra help to breastfeed. He's likely to be less able to attach because of the effect on his reflexes – see page 78 for what you can do to help your baby become interested in feeding.

Type of delivery

Sometimes, a difficult birth with a long labour can mean your baby is tired at birth, and less able to stay alert and interested in feeding.

Mothers who gave birth by caesarean (now about 25 per cent of births) used to be told to expect a delay in getting breastfeeding underway as it was thought that their milk 'came in' later. But this is now known not to be the case. If you are having an elective caesarean, or if one becomes necessary during labour, it should not affect your milk production, although you may need help with positioning the baby while your scar is still tender.

If an emergency caesarean becomes necessary, and you are both healthy after the birth, there's no reason why you cannot hold your baby skin-to-skin straight away. However, there is a routine tendency in many maternity units to wrap babies up in blankets after a caesarean, so you might have to ask in advance – and get it written into your notes – if you don't want this to happen.

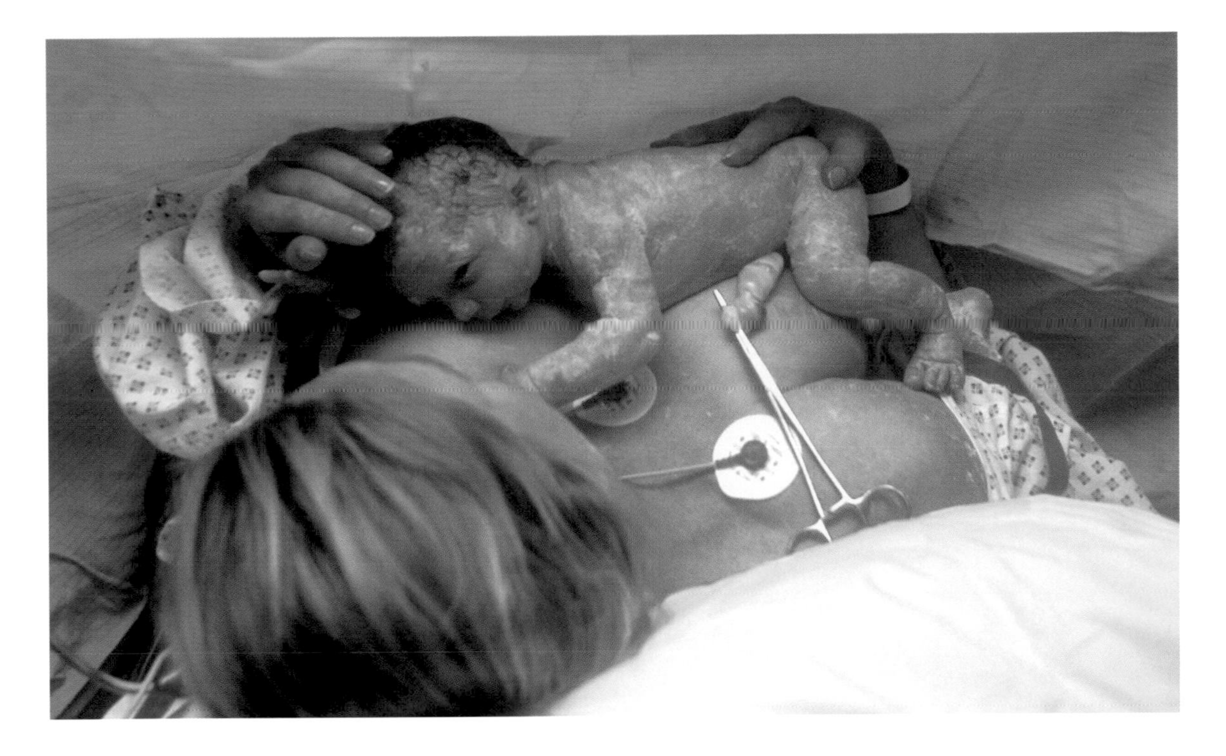

You will certainly need help in holding the baby close: you're likely to be dressed in a fastened-up-the-back theatre gown and unable to sit up as the surgeon may be stitching you at this point; you will also probably have a drip in your arm.

Twins

Caesarean sections are more common with twin births so you'll find moving into a comfortable position and holding one or both new babies is very difficult to do without someone actively assisting you in the first week or so. Even if you have not had a section, extra help will be essential until you become more adept. Twins usually weigh less at birth and are more likely to be pre-term, so the nutrients in breast milk provide them with what they need for the brain growth that would have happened in the uterus. It also protects them against infection.

Staying together

Whatever the setbacks to a smooth and straightforward birth, they don't have to mean a difficult start to breastfeeding. Keeping close to your baby, and not restricting breastfeeding by limiting it, timing it or scheduling it should get things off to a good start, as long as both you and your baby are healthy. And even if there are health problems, or you have to be separated because one or both of you needs treatment or observation, then you can go some way to making up for this – see pages 78–9 for suggestions on this. Mothers have successfully established breastfeeding after quite long periods of separation. Ask the hospital for a breastfeeding specialist who can help you overcome your own individual challenges.

Hospital routines

Maternity units should all be working within guidelines laid down by the UNICEF/WHO Baby Friendly initiative. Studies show that babies born in a Baby Friendly hospital are more likely to start breastfeeding and to breastfeed for longer than babies born in a hospital without the award.

In a hospital that's Baby Friendly, or working towards it, you and your baby will be encouraged to stay close. You should not be advised to give any formula or water or anything else, unless your baby is considered to need it for a medical reason. You'll be supported to respond to your baby's feeding needs as often as he shows them.

Nevertheless, in reality, mothers sometimes say they didn't get good support and information in hospital, even where there are good policies in place and even with full Baby Friendly accreditation. Some mothers have been told they're feeding 'too often' or are not told that holding their baby and feeding to comfort him are good things. Jaundice can be a cause of sleepiness in babies, and make them a little less interested in feeding, so it's even more important for them to have every opportunity to do so. If a baby is sleepy, or reluctant to feed or seems not to know how to attach himself to the breast, 'help' may involve a degree of

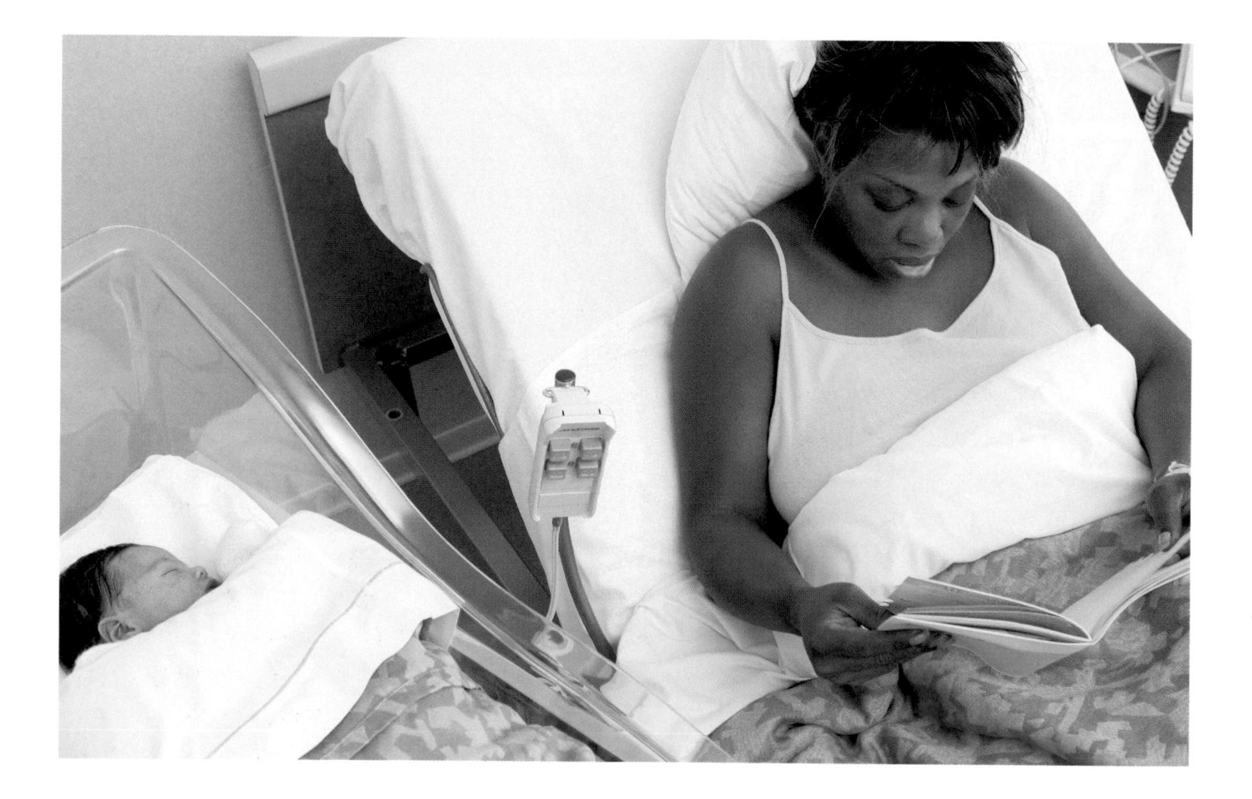

BABIES NEEDING SPECIAL CARE

If your baby needs medical care or observation after birth, you can still breastfeed. Very pre-term babies (younger than about 34–36 weeks gestation) may need to be given expressed milk by tube (milk is dripped down a narrow tube inserted into the baby's nose). The very smallest of pre-term babies (from about 23–26 weeks) may need parenteral feeding which bypasses the stomach and delivers a nutrient solution directly into the bloodstream by a drip. Twins and other multiples are more likely than singletons to be born early, and have similar problems with feeding.

If your baby (or babies) is not able to breastfeed right away, you should be encouraged to express your milk (see page 106). You should start doing this as soon as you can – certainly on the first day, if this is at all possible. Frequent and regular expressing – at least 8 to 10 times in 24 hours including overnight – is hard work and time-consuming, but it's important. Make it clear to hospital staff that you want to do this: you may need to ask them to wake you during the night.

Removing milk 'primes' your body's breastfeeding 'production line', so you'll have the milk there in your breasts when your baby is well enough to use it.

After some days, you will probably get more breast milk than your baby will need, and build up a stock of frozen milk. That's fine – you can use it later (see page 75) or donate it to the hospital's milk bank.

manhandling of breast and baby. This may feel disempowering to the mother and may upset the baby. Support for a crying baby with an exhausted mother may consist of suggesting a bottle of formula as a solution.

In addition, genuine problems with breastfeeding may not be spotted in hospital. A baby who is not transferring milk from breast to mouth effectively may be missed. In fact, the mother may be told all is well, and it's only days later at home that it becomes clear the baby is not feeding well at all. A baby at the breast may look as if he's feeding, but nothing much is actually happening by way of milk being transferred from breast to baby. There are ways to check your baby is feeding well – see pages 78–9 for guidance on what to do if you suspect he is not getting enough (or any) milk.

If you're not happy with the way breastfeeding is going, or you're worried about advice you've been given, you can ask to see the infant feeding specialist. Most maternity units have a designated healthcare professional in this role – almost always a senior midwife. He or she

KANGAROO CARE

A whole body of research shows measurable advantages for both baby and mother of kangaroo care. From the very start, pre-term or sick babies can usually be cared for in this way. The name comes from the way a baby is snuggled up close to a carer (usually the mother), inside her clothing or a wrap, which holds him close to her skin, pressed up against her chest. Any tubes or monitoring devices normally remain in place.

This form of care has been shown to be very beneficial in a range of ways, including temperature control and stabilising of the baby's heart and respiration rates, and it has powerful psychological and emotional benefits, too.

The 'getting to know you' cuddling that mothers of term babies can take for granted, and which is so much a part of the early mother–baby relationship, is replicated by kangaroo care. Mothers who can be in touch (literally) with their babies in this way feel their babies belong to them and not to the hospital staff. This boosts confidence and eases the normal, understandable wariness parents may feel around a tiny, vulnerable baby.

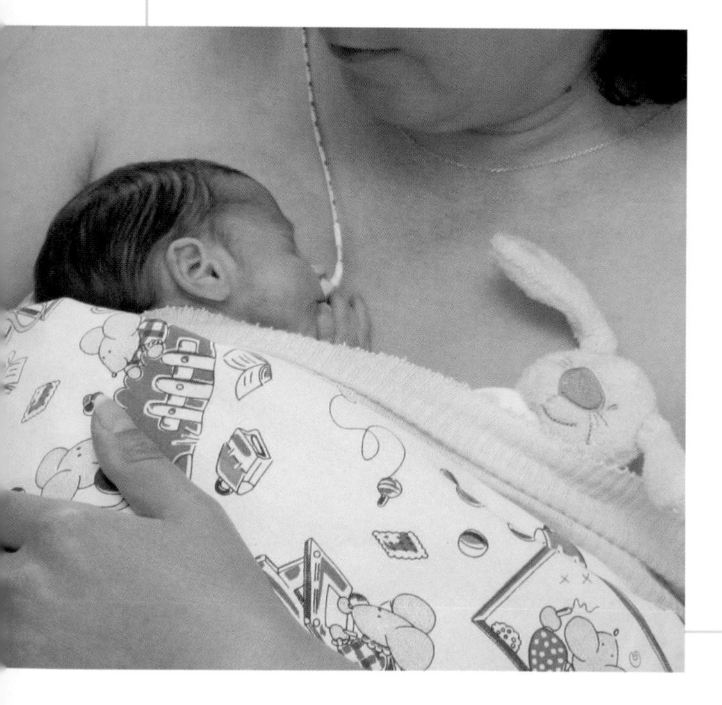

You'll be encouraged to place your arms and hands very gently against your baby, and to avoid actual patting or stroking, which can be disturbing and over-stimulating to him. In the uterus – where he would normally be at this age – the environment is warm, constant, muffled and enclosing so it's understandable tiny babies react best to something that mimics this.

If you're able to give your baby kangaroo care, you'll find it promotes your breast milk production. The ability to co-ordinate sucking and swallowing, and the muscular strength needed to make the jaw, mouth and tongue work together, are not apparent until 35–36 weeks of gestation, so even though your baby can't actually suck and swallow, your body's hormonal response is stimulated, making milk production and expressing easier.

Fathers can give kangaroo care too. The human contact soothes the baby and it's also a way for fathers to connect emotionally with their babies.

has had extra training and developed an expertise in early-days feeding.

If you go home very soon after the birth, as many women do now (figures show that about a fifth of women go home the day they give birth and 90 per cent are home in three days or less), stay close to your baby. The community midwife should visit you soon after you go home, and you can share any concerns with her, just as you would in hospital.

Donor milk

If you are unable to make sufficient breast milk or express often enough to get a good supply, you may want to take advantage of donor milk from other mothers. There is usually a milk bank linked to the special care baby unit. Donor milk is screened and pooled by the milk bank, then pasteurised so you can be sure it's safe.

Informal milk sharing – when one mother donates her expressed breast milk to another mother directly – seems to be on the increase, despite some safety issues. If you are depending on donor milk, you need to be confident the donor does not smoke or use street drugs, is not taking any medication that is incompatible with breastfeeding, and is not HIV positive. Her general hygiene also needs to be good. Internet milk-sharing sites offer to put mothers in touch with one another if they have no immediate contacts, but as with anyone you meet over the web, use all your adult common sense to check out they are who, and what, they say they are.

BOTTLEFEEDING CONSIDERATIONS

If you choose to bottlefeed your baby from birth, the hospital in which you deliver should adhere to Baby Friendly principles and encourage you and your baby to stay close and help you to respond to your baby's cues (see page 55) when he needs feeding.

Your own health and breastfeeding

Very few health conditions impact on breastfeeding, but there are some considerations.

- If you are on long-term medication check whether you need to alter the type or the dose. If you're told 'you can't breastfeed' ask what the risks actually are. Many women are advised to stop, or not even to start, when it isn't necessary. There are good sources of information so talk to your doctor about your options. Some drugs used to treat serious mental illness, or cancer, may not be compatible with breastfeeding. If you need drug treatment for postnatal depression, there are several which have been shown to be safe in use. Very few drugs truly rule out breastfeeding.
- Separation from your baby means breastfeeding may get off to a slower, and more difficult, start. If you are separated after breastfeeding has begun because you need treatment, you should express to maintain your comfort and your milk supply.
- Some physical disabilities may mean you need extra help to breastfeed comfortably. Women who have missing limbs or restricted use of their limbs can breastfeed, and the support organisations for specific disabilities can be a good source of practical advice and support from other mothers who have faced the same challenges.
- Serious bleeding after the birth (post-partum haemorrhage) can make it harder to build up a milk supply – you may need to feed your baby more often and/or express milk to build your supply. A few women who have had bleeding develop Sheehan's syndrome, which affects the pituitary gland (the gland which governs the hormones involved in milk production). These women may find they have little or no breast milk. Sheehan's syndrome can usually be treated, but often its symptoms are missed. The condition is diagnosed by a blood test.
- A retained placenta – where parts of the placenta still adhere to the wall of the uterus – can also impact on milk supply. The retained parts can be removed under anaesthetic.

This is not an exhaustive list of possible conditions that can affect your milk production, and if you have an unexplained reason for breastfeeding difficulties or supply problems, it's worth getting a referral from your doctor for specialist advice. You can then be examined for the rare underlying causes of poor milk production, and treated when this is possible.

Sometimes mothers worry that if they are ill with something like food poisoning, an infection or a fever, they should stop or suspend breastfeeding, to prevent their baby picking up the same bug. This is not necessary. Breast milk is not a vehicle for pathogens – HIV is the only illness which has been shown to pass from mother to baby through breast milk.

TONGUE TIE

Some babies (the number varies between 0.4 per cent and as many as 10 per cent, depending on which study you read) are born with ankyloglossia, more commonly known as tongue tie. In tongue tie, the frenulum, the little piece of skin joining the tongue to the bottom of the mouth, is short, thick or otherwise positioned close to the end of the tongue. This restricts movement and therefore the baby's ability to attach to the breast and feed effectively. The result can be sore nipples for you, and very painful feeding, frustration and hunger for your baby. A 'posterior tongue tie' means the frenulum is further back, but because it anchors the tongue too tightly for free movement, the baby still has difficulty attaching.

Babies sometimes compensate for their attachment problems by clamping on the nipple, which might enable them to stay on for longer, but which can cause serious pain and nipple damage.

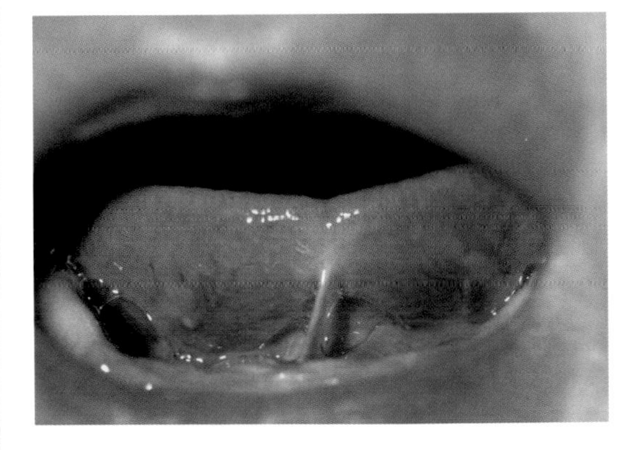

We're still learning about tongue tie and its effects, and whether or not all babies with the condition need treating. Treatment is a short, quick and painless operation which 'snips' the frenulum and allows freer movement. It's normally done without anaesthetic and the baby hardly even notices it happening. Your midwife, doctor or health visitor should know who does this procedure in your area.

Post-op, some babies feed perfectly well and everything is just fine. However, this is not the case every time. Some babies need a second 'snip' and some babies seem to need time to learn to attach in a comfortable way. In others, it may be that tongue tie was not causing the problem after all.

This is a changing field of study and treatment, but there is agreement that if tongue tie is causing a problem, early treatment is important. It can take years for a child's frenulum to stretch naturally, if it does at all, so waiting for things to work themselves out is not the answer.

Tongue tie (here in a month-old baby) can cause problems with breastfeeding and, later if untreated, with speech.

BABY WHO WON'T BREASTFEED

If your baby does not want to feed, it can be demoralising and baffling and cause a lot of upset, especially if you're tired, uncomfortable and under-confident.

In newborns, reluctance to feed might be a result of a difficult birth, or some rough handling by helpers who have done a bit too much 'pushing and shoving' to get the baby on the breast. It can also be caused by bad timing – waking the baby up to feed can sometimes turn the baby right off so he falls asleep again.

A baby might show his reluctance to breastfeed by arching his back away when he's

BABYMOON

With a baby of any age, including a newborn, a 'babymoon' can often bring about a real change, and it's nice to do even if your baby's feeding well. It needs some organising, especially if you have other children to care for, so you'll need support from your partner, family or close friends. Just take your baby into bed with you, and stay there, being waited on if you can. Don't expect your baby to sleep or rest apart from you, and don't do much, if anything, except feeding (yourself as well – someone should bring you food and drink) and gazing and holding. Watching TV or listening to the radio or some music is fine, of course, as well. Plenty of cultures, including our own until recently, accept and embrace the idea of the mother and baby having quiet time together, with the household chores taken over by other people. The peace and comfort of the babymoon is a tradition we could happily restart in the 21st century.

placed near the breast, by crying and turning his head away, or sometimes, by 'switching off' and falling asleep after no more than a few seconds.

Here's what can turn things around:

- Patience, gentleness and less direct manhandling of the baby's head and body (holding and cuddling are fine).
- Biological nurturing positions (see page 58) which enable self-attachment – try doing this in the bath, ensuring your baby stays warm by slooshing water over his back and keep his upper body out of the water. (If there is any chance you might fall asleep, have someone else in the room with you.)
- Responding to early feeding cues such as mouth movements, hand movements, head movements (see page 55) – try to get in with the offer of a feed before your baby starts crying.

If your baby is still learning to take the breast effectively, you'll need to express to maintain your supply. Your baby can have the milk in a bottle or in a small cup held up to his mouth (egg cups are fine, or you can buy feeding cups for young babies). You might have heard of 'nipple confusion' – it's sometimes thought that babies who take bottle teats then become unable to feed from the breast. There's hardly any research on this, and many experienced breastfeeding supporters feel the worry is overstated. If the breast milk supply is kept up so it's rewarding for babies when they do come to the breast, they are likely to come back to it. The rejection of the breast is not confusion so much as a choice for the productive bottle rather than the unproductive breast.

Long-term resistance to the breast for no apparent reason is rare, but it does happen, and it's very dispiriting. However, babies do sometimes surprise everyone, sometimes after weeks, and all becomes well. They manage an effective feed, and never look back. The trouble is, there is no way of predicting which babies will do so.

With older babies, fighting at the breast or outright refusal in other ways could be a 'nursing strike'. Babies of a few months old might show this behaviour after a period of happy breastfeeding. Sometimes, you can pinpoint an incident which might have caused it – perhaps the baby was frightened by a loud noise while he was feeding or has become confused and unsettled by being left with an unfamiliar carer. More often you can't discern a reason. You can get things back to the way they were by:

- using the suggestions for a young baby, as above;
- feeding when your baby is sleepy or even almost asleep;
- feeding standing up or in some other position you rarely use (the oddity of this appears to make a baby forget whatever objection he had).

Just occasionally, an ear infection, which involves pain in one or both ears can lead to an apparent strike. Your doctor can quickly diagnose and treat an infection.

Breastfeeding and pain

It's absolutely not a given that breastfeeding is painful for everyone or even most women. Don't accept that 'it always hurts' and ignore people who tell you 'just persevere – it will get better'. A certain amount of tenderness is very common and may be the result of your nipples getting used to the new sensations. In the first days when the milk 'comes in', breasts can be swollen and sensitive. Known as engorgement, this condition can make it difficult for a baby to feed, but tends to resolve as the 'supply and demand' nature of breastfeeding becomes established (see page 52). Pain that gets worse rather than better over a day or so is not 'normal' and may be an indication that something needs putting right.

Sometimes, pain resolves itself spontaneously. A baby may learn to open wider, or a mum comes up with ways of making things feel better. But pain is not something you need to put up with in the hope that by doing nothing, all will be well. A supportive, expert eye can often help you to change a painful, frustrating experience into a happy and easy one.

Sore nipples

Check that your baby is attached well to your breast; as well as the nipple, he should have a good mouthful of the areola too. Sometimes a baby looks as if he's well attached but it isn't actually the case. If your baby is latched on properly (see page 57), and he should be able to do so without his tongue getting in the way, feeding should be pain-free.

Think about the shape of a baby's mouth – the hard palate forms a dome inside. This allows your baby to use his tongue to draw in your breast, so the nipple points down his throat. He then 'milks' your breast with his tongue and lower jaw (see pages 56–57). If your nipple appears flattened on the top when it comes out of your baby's mouth (rather like the shape of a new lipstick), it has been compressed between your baby's tongue and hard palate. If your nipple appears grazed, or has tiny blood blisters or a red stripe on it, or is cracked or bleeding, it

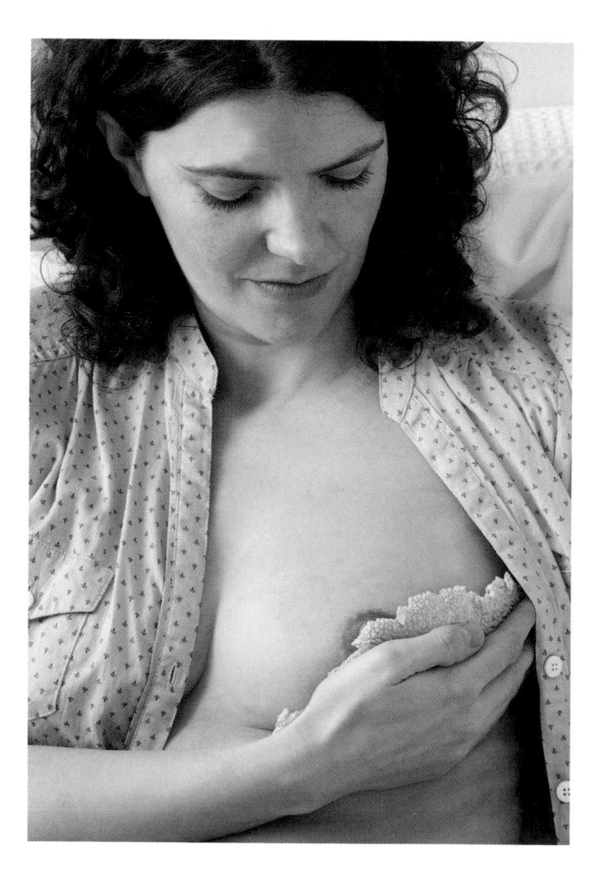

has also been compressed. In all these cases, you will almost certainly be in pain, and in some cases, your baby may have to work hard to get an effective feed (though plenty of babies thrive and enjoy feeding, even when not attached comfortably).

Cracked or grazed nipples need healing treatment as well as changes in your baby's position and attachment. 'Moist wound healing' which means applying a product that does not allow a scab to form is often very effective; ask your chemist to recommend something. These lotions and ointments are normally safe for your baby to ingest, so you don't need to wipe them off before feeding again, but check the package to make sure.

Try feeding your baby in a different position (see pages 58–59 for your options) and check for tongue tie (see page 77).

Occasionally, the fungal infection thrush can affect the nipples and make them sore with hard-to-heal cracks. Your doctor can prescribe anti-fungal medication for you and for your baby (who needs treating whether he has symptoms or not).

Painful breasts

Red patches or lumps, or a swollen area in the breast may indicate a blocked duct. This happens when milk remains in the breast, effectively clogging it up. Sometimes, you can see a white spot blocking one of the exit holes where the milk leaves the nipple. Mastitis, an inflammation or infection of the breast, can result from a persistently blocked duct. If you suspect you have a blocked duct, your first aim is to get milk flowing through the affected part. You can do this by feeding first on that side, and by offering that breast more often. Massage – be gentle if there is any pain – directly over the area can help. If the self-help does not work within a day or so, or if you feel ill, with flu-like symptoms or a fever, see your doctor. You may have infective rather than solely inflammatory mastitis and you may be offered antibiotics to reduce the inflammation and prevent, or treat, the infection.

Repeated mastitis/blocked ducts need some detective work. Are you wearing a bra or other clothing, or using a position at night perhaps, that puts pressure on a particular area of the breast, and affects drainage? Could it be you need a longer course of antibiotics so the same infection does not recur all the time? A breastfeeding counsellor or specialist might be able to explore other possible causes with you. A few women just seem susceptible to repeat instances of the condition and then, as time passes, they have fewer occurrences.

If you're very unlucky, your mastitis may become an abscess – a collection of pus where the blockage was, which appears as a large, sometimes shiny swelling and may or may not be painful. Antibiotics may get rid of it, but you may have to go to hospital for a procedure to drain it under local anaesthetic. You can usually continue to breastfeed once the drain and any dressing have been removed, though the area may remain a little tender for a while.

When the milk comes in engorgement – swelling of the breasts caused by the pressure of new milk and expanding blood vessels – is common. A traditional remedy is to insert a cabbage leaf into the bra to relieve discomfort.

Breastfeeding and milk supply

One of the most common worries, and among the most common reasons for stopping breastfeeding, is the question of milk supply. If a breastfed baby seems fussy or cries, or does not settle to sleep, or does not sleep for long, sooner or later, someone – if not the mother herself – will question whether he is getting enough milk.

The concern comes partly from the way we are used to measuring and quantifying everything but also from a very strong need to know our babies are growing and healthy. You can't see the breast milk reaching a baby's stomach and neither a baby's abdomen nor your breasts have any calibrations showing fluid ounces or millilitres. You just have to trust that what's needed is being made and going in. Actually, calibrations wouldn't help as appetite and need differ from baby to baby, but there's something comforting about knowing exactly how much is going in.

Generally speaking, a baby who's gaining weight as expected, showing signs of being contented and healthy, is developing normally and producing several wet nappies a day is being well-fed. In the first week, you can check he is producing urine by placing a cotton wool ball in the nappy, as modern disposables absorb urine very well. Counting nappies is not really possible, as babies urinate many times a day. With a young baby, almost every nappy you remove is likely to

BOTTLEFEEDING CONSIDERATIONS

Worrying about whether a bottlefed baby is getting enough milk is less of a concern. However, if you are told your baby does need more formula and it is difficult to make him feed, try feeding little and often – smaller amounts more frequently.

TOO MUCH MILK?

If your breasts are almost always uncomfortably full, if your baby is gaining weight very fast (climbing up the centile charts rather than staying close to the same line, see page 134), if he seems uncomfortable after or between feeds, if he is sometimes desperate to feed and then pulls off spluttering, it could be both of you are having to cope with your over-generous milk supply. Some mothers are very bountiful, and make more milk than their babies actually ask for, sometimes far more milk. These signs often become noticeable from the age of about five or six weeks. If you think this may be the cause of your baby's fussiness and squirming, try reducing your supply by deliberately feeding on one breast only in every period of four or five (or perhaps as long as six) hours. This is called 'block nursing'. Every time you feed your baby within this period, you use the same breast. If the other unused breast becomes very uncomfortable, gentle and minimal hand expressing will keep things within bounds. You should see a difference in a couple of days or so.

show signs that your baby has passed urine. A reassuring sign of sufficient milk in the first weeks is regular stools – at least three a day after about day 5. (After the first weeks, this is not such a reliable sign, as many babies can go several days without passing a stool, without there being any problem at all with milk supply.)

If you are worried at all whether your baby is getting enough milk – and it does happen that some babies don't get enough and that some mothers have to work hard at maintaining a good supply – the easiest and most effective way of increasing your baby's intake, and your milk supply, is to feed more often. Easy ways to increase your supply and your baby's intake include:

- Offering the other breast when your baby seems to have lost interest in one of them, then going back again for a further 'turn' at the first one, and then back to the second, and so on (this is called switch nursing).
- Trying breast compression when your baby appears to have finished. Place your thumb on one side of your breast and your fingers on the other and gently press together. This makes a further mouthful of breast milk available, and may pique his interest to feed more. It also further removes milk which boosts your supply.
- Keeping your baby close to you day and night and responding to every feeding cue (mouth, head and hand movements, see page 55).
- Expressing milk between breastfeeds, if necessary, as this is extra stimulation for the breasts. Give your supply a few days to increase and when you feel things are back on track, you can reduce the intensity.

Social and cultural constraints

Breastfeeding has evolved with the human species, and while it may not always be easy, happy or comfortable for every individual, as a physical process it's not ever going to go away. But socially and culturally, it's a different story. Could breastfeeding be incompatible with women's lives today?

The breastfeeding experience can cause apparent conflict for many reasons:

- The need or the desire to work outside the home, with few or no opportunities to continue breastfeeding actually in the workplace.
- Expectations that bottlefeeding is more 'normal' and that it's a bit weird or somehow perverse to breastfeed after the baby reaches a particular age or stage, or even to breastfeed at all.
- Lack, or the perceived lack, of acceptance of breastfeeding in a public place, or in front of other people anywhere, even your own home.
- The needs of other children or family members which don't always allow a baby to be responded to quickly.

Being well-informed about how breastfeeding works can combat the idea that it's not normal to breastfeed. But it can feel like a conflict if the demands of your adult life and its inevitable responsibilities interfere with the needs of your baby. Babies don't respect a work timetable or your having to take and/or collect an older sibling from school.

Breastfeeding does not inevitably set up an irresolvable conflict, as long as supportive structures are in place. A realistic maternity leave, which ensures women don't lose out financially by taking time off from work, means a baby can be fully breastfed for several months, and that breastfeeding can continue alongside other foods (served up by other carers) afterwards.

People who object to the sight of breastfeeding should have no power over the mother who breastfeeds in public. Legislation can protect mothers from anyone who suggests they breastfeed elsewhere or stop altogether. Greater acceptance of, and knowledge about, breastfeeding means family and friends should expect to help with other children and household tasks for a time, though legislation on that is never going to be possible.

If it's accepted that breastfeeding is a worthwhile choice, then it demands more than a mother's own decision to do it. Employment conditions, equality laws and any other necessary social structures should be in place to enable this choice to be made in the first place, and to enable it to continue for as long as the mother chooses. There should be no need to stop because of a return to work or education.

The notion that childcare can be shared between the sexes is perfectly workable, too. The fact that this one aspect of feeding can't be divided in a literal way doesn't have to undermine that, either. Men have a role in enabling breastfeeding, by taking over other tasks for the few short months a baby has nothing else to eat or drink – and then share in meal preparation and serving when the menu expands.

Other Western societies, notably all the Scandinavian countries, have high levels of breastfeeding initiation and maintenance, and high levels of female employment. But they do have flexible employment conditions, and maternity (and paternity) leave, and no one there would dream of thinking breastfeeding was anything but an unremarkable sight.

Breastfeeding away from home

It's easier to breastfeed than bottlefeed when you're travelling, visiting, shopping or doing anything that takes you and your baby out into the wider world. There's no extra equipment and preparation is zero – no looking for kettles or warmers or water to mix powder.

Your feelings of comfort at being seen by other people are going to be personal to you, and you might change your mind as you become more experienced and more used to breastfeeding wherever you and your baby happen to be. Some women are shy of strangers seeing them; some women are fine about strangers but feel awkward in front of family and friends – or perhaps some family and friends only. And at the other end of the spectrum, some mothers never give it a thought, and always feel fine about it, any time, anywhere.

In the UK, maternity legislation (up to six months postnatal) and sex equality legislation (after six months) mean no one has the right to stop you breastfeeding in a public place, and in Scotland, it's actually an offence to even try.

Legislation is one thing, however, and your feelings about your own comfort are another.

To make feeding easier, at home or on the move, choose separates you can slide down (top) or lift up (left) to allow your baby access to your breasts. Carrying your baby in a sling (right) makes feeding easy on the move and can help you to feed 'under wraps' if that is what you prefer.

You may feel sensitive to other people's criticisms, or expectations of you to 'be discreet'. It's clear some people have difficulty in accepting 'public' breastfeeding, as whenever the topic comes up for discussion in the media, some quite astonishing opinions are on display – far more openly and far more indiscreetly than any brief sight of female flesh could be.

Dressing for easy feeding

If you feel better keeping yourself under wraps in public, you can become more confident by wearing clothing that's easy to manage. This usually means separates and a 'layered' approach with a vest top you can lift up rather than opening down the centre, plus a bra with cups that open or drop down singly. Smaller breasted women can lift a breast over the top of an ordinary bra.

You might get quite clever with a shawl or a pashmina, and some mothers get creative with scarves, though older babies become very resistant to feeding in the dark and quite adept at pulling off your carefully constructed modesty device (but by that time you'll probably care a lot less than you did at first). Internet traders offer 'nursing covers' or ponchos which are like gigantic bibs covering the baby's head and your chest. There are also baby hats with a huge brim sold for the same purpose. Again, a baby over a few months may not tolerate these things, and they look so unusual, you might as well wear a placard announcing 'Warning: baby feeding here. Please don't look.'

CHAPTER 6

Getting started with bottlefeeding

Bottlefeeding has its own list of practical dos and don'ts, to ensure that it is done effectively and safely, as well as things you can do to make life easier for yourself and your family while feeding. If you choose to bottlefeed, you must bear in mind that it is more than just a way of nourishing your baby; it is also an important part of her social and emotional care.

Bottlefeeding is not limited to formula feeding; it is often used to give expressed breast milk and can be used in conjunction with breastfeeding in a practice known as 'mixed feeding'. To do this successfully, however, needs some planning, and this is discussed more in depth in the next chapter, together with reasons why you might choose to feed your baby in this way.

Bottlefeeding is a normal and everyday occurrence but not all women are happy using bottles – for some women, not being able to breastfeed (for whatever reason) is a disappointment and source of sadness – and sometimes a woman meets with hostile reactions or even overt and explicit criticism if she bottlefeeds. It's easy for people to assume you feel okay about bottlefeeding, even if your own feelings are negative or at least mixed, and this chapter also explores how you might cope with bottle/formula feeding when you are facing difficulties.

What you need to bottlefeed

If you are fully bottlefeeding your baby, you need several bottles and several teats – half a dozen of each is usually recommended. You can make do with fewer but this number allows you to clean and sterilise a batch of bottles and teats at a time, maybe once a day, and to always have a clean bottle and teat available when you need one.

If you are using formula (see pages 40–41 for a description of different types), you will need a supply the milk of your choice. If you are giving your baby expressed breast milk, you will probably need a breast pump. This is not absolutely essential, as you can hand express very effectively once you get the knack, but many women find a pump makes things quicker, especially if they express more than just occasionally (see pages 106–7).

You will also need cleaning equipment, such as a bottle brush for bottles and teats, and equipment for sterilising (you have a number of choices here – see page 94).

Bottle and teat technology moves on all the time, and many manufacturers make marketing claims for your baby's comfort, or their products' powers against colic or similarity to breast milk. You'll probably develop your own preference, as will your baby – and some babies are very fussy indeed.

Bottles

There are a number of different bottles on the market. In the UK and many other countries, all new feeding bottles are 'BPA free', which means the polycarbonate plastic used in their manufacture contains no bisphenol A. This chemical has caused concern for many years because of its links to adverse health effects, principally on hormones. Glass bottles are hard to find these days, but you can buy them on the internet. Young babies only take small amounts of milk at each feed so bottles holding up to 125 ml capacity will suffice. However, if you wish, you can start out with the larger 240-ml-sized bottles.

Anti-colic bottles and teats use a valve designed to prevent air in the bottle or teat getting into the baby – some parents report that this is effective and seems to lead to less discomfort after feeds, but others report no difference at all. It's not always certain – by a long way – that air ('wind') in the baby's stomach is the cause of the unexplained crying we term 'colic'.

Bottles are available with a heat sensor, which indicates when the milk is too hot. This feature is not essential, but could be useful if you have poor sensitivity to heat or cold.

Disposable, single-use, all-in-one bottles and teats come ready to use in packs of four or five. They are expensive for everyday use but handy for odd occasions or when travelling to use with cartons of ready-to-feed formula.

An alternative to conventional reusable bottles are pre-sterilised, disposable plastic liners which sit inside a plastic holder – you fill the liner with milk, and as the baby removes the milk, the liner collapses. The idea here is that the baby swallows less air. They can be a convenient way of bottlefeeding away from home if you can't sterilise bottles easily.

Do not use

- Worn or scratched bottles as they are difficult to clean properly.
- Older bottles, perhaps from a previous child, or bottles that have been passed on to you, as they may contain bisphenol A (see opposite).
- Teats that have become sticky or cracked.

Teats

Choosing the right teat is generally down to your baby's preference and it normally takes a bit of trial and error to get the right one. Young babies tend to feed best on 'newborn' flow teats, which you can swap for medium flow as your baby grows, moving up to fast flow when your baby can cope. Again, trial and error are needed to get the right one.

Teats are made from latex or silicone. Latex is softer (which some babies prefer) but silicone is longer lasting. Although many teats are a standard size and fit a variety of bottles, some only fit their own bottles, so be careful to check the packaging before buying. 'Ordinary' teats are holed at the exit point but some are cross cut. Additionally, some are labelled 'orthodontic' and claim to support normal jaw development; others claim to make bottlefeeding feel like breastfeeding; still others enable a varied flow, so if you turn the bottle through 180 degrees the flow changes. Some are vented, to take air away from the baby while others let air in, to prevent the teat from collapsing and blocking the flow. There isn't any convincing evidence that one teat is better than another, or indeed more like breastfeeding, but different types do have their fan clubs.

Preparing formula and bottles

Cleanliness and careful preparation of a formula feed are important for your baby's health and safety. A baby who is given formula milk won't get the protective antibodies present in breast milk and may be exposed to pathogens that can cause infection. Dried formula, for example, may contain bacteria including salmonella and a specific bacterium called *Enterobacter sakazakii*. (This is not an issue, however, with ready-to-feed formula milk, which comes in cartons and is heat-treated and sterile.) Babies fed on formula milk are more likely to suffer from gastroenteritis, respiratory infections and ear infections. You need to ensure that bottles of formula are prepared carefully and hygienically to reduce the risks, and make bottlefeeding safer for your baby. It doesn't have to be obsessive or anxiety-making, but it should be consistent, so you get into good habits. You need a routine with the way you prepare formula, and one with the way you care for the equipment you use. These hygiene rules apply whether you are using formula or expressed breast milk.

Making up formula

Ask your midwife or health visitor for a leaflet you can keep in your kitchen as a handy reminder of what to do until you get used to the routine. It's a good idea to share this with anyone who might prepare bottles for you, as the advice on water temperature has changed in recent years. There are also instructions on tins or packets of formula.

There are two basic steps to preparing a bottle of formula – and your leaflet and the on-pack instructions will remind you to do this on a clean surface and with clean hands.

First, take a clean bottle and, using water that has been boiled and which is not less than 70°C, pour in the required amount (this usually

means using water boiled in the last 30 minutes). Then add the required number of scoops of powdered formula to the bottle. Replace the lid or teat on the bottle, then add the retaining ring (the plastic that goes round the neck of the bottle and holds the teat on) and screw tightly. Hold the teat by its edge as you place it on the top of the bottle, so your fingers don't come into contact with the end. Gently tip the bottle up and down a few times to dissolve the powder. Cool by standing the bottle in cold water or running it under the cold tap. Check the milk is not too hot before you give it to your baby. Shake a few drops on to your wrist – it should feel no more than slightly warm.

Formula milk is best made up and given to a baby straight away, as this reduces the risk of bacteria multiplying and causing illness. Current guidelines from the UK's Department of Health – and from UNICEF – recommend that young and/or vulnerable (sick, pre-term or otherwise compromised) babies should have freshly made formula milk, or else ready-to-feed formula, decanted from the carton into a clean, sterilised bottle.

For practical purposes, it's very difficult to make every feed as and when your baby needs it, especially

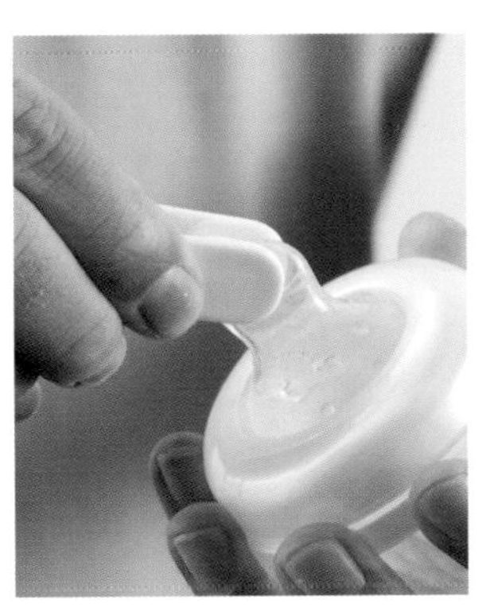

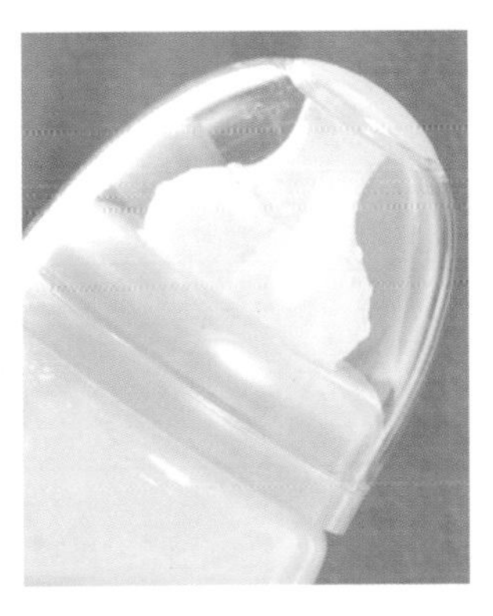

if your baby is feeding unpredictably. Current guidelines for healthy, term babies allow for storage of made-up bottles for up to 24 hours, at the back of the fridge (where it's coldest), as long as they are made up correctly in the first instance. Keep the bottle closed (bottles come with little discs that keep the top sealed), or if you store it with the teat on, use the cover that comes with the bottle for this purpose.

Many parents make up a number of bottles of milk at a time, perhaps a day's worth, or half a day's worth, and store them in the fridge until they're needed. Talk it over with your health visitor. One approach is to offer ready-to-feed or freshly made formula when your baby is new, say up to a month old, and then to switch to making up bottles in advance when your baby is older.

Cleaning and sterilising

Because warm milk is a breeding ground for bacteria, thorough cleaning of bottles, teats, and all the other accoutrements like covers and lids, is very important. In the UK, sterilising is advised, using whatever method is convenient for you. In other countries, the advice is to use thorough hand washing and brushing followed by washing on the hot cycle in a dishwasher, leaving the items to dry as the steam evaporates.

Non-dishwasher methods

You have a choice of methods – none rated better or more efficient than the other – so your choice will depend on expense, ease of use and, possibly, space. Manufacturers continue to make changes in the design and functionality of sterilising equipment. Check out forums and parenting websites for user reports of different methods and information on developments.

Electric steam steriliser

A purpose-built electric unit sits on your kitchen top. It takes only a few minutes and stores the equipment clean until you need to use it.

Microwavable unit

You place your equipment inside and allow the microwave to do the rest. Again, it's quick (a few minutes), and you store the equipment in most units as well.

Cold water tank

A tank (or a large container) holds your bottles and equipment under water. You need sterilising liquid or tablets, which dissolve in the water, and your equipment needs to be kept in it for 30 minutes. You may need to rinse bottles and teats in cooled boiled water to get rid of the taste of the sterilising solution.

Boiling water

You can use a sufficiently large saucepan to boil the items for 10 minutes. Obviously, you'll need to take care getting them out of the water unless you leave them until the water cools down.

Formula know-how

You can read an overview of the different sorts of formula available today in chapter 3, pages 40–1.

Which to choose

Deciding which formula to use for your baby is something you can discuss with your midwife or health visitor. Unless your baby has special dietary needs, selecting a brand can be done on the basis of what you can buy easily and locally (in case you run out and need to replenish quickly). Choosing a type of formula depends on the age of your baby but first-stage infant formula is safe for all ages, and if you're happy with this, there is no need to change.

It is commonly thought that you shouldn't change formula brands and your baby should remain on the same brand all the time he has formula. There's no justification for this or evidence that a change is too much of an onslaught on a baby's system. Plenty of parents do change brands – usually because their baby suffers from diarrhoea, constipation or pain with wind after feeds and swapping brands is a reasonable response to this. While these symptoms might not be due to the formula, and you can talk about them with your health visitor, a change in brand is worth a try if your baby suffers from any of these problems and things don't improve.

There are brands labelled 'easy digest' or 'comfort' for babies who have repeated minor digestive disturbances. The difference with these formulas is usually that the protein has been broken down more than with regular formula,

so it becomes easier for the baby to digest. In addition, prebiotics (substances that stimulate digestion) in the formula help the formation of softer, easier-to-pass, stools.

How much to give

Formula-fed babies can't be expected to take a pre-determined amount of milk at every feed, and the guidance on amounts on every formula pack should be used very flexibly – your baby is the best guide. A rule of thumb is to expect your baby to take something like 150 grams per kilo of body weight in a 24-hour period; in imperial measures, that works out as 2½ fluid ounces per pound. But in practice, healthy babies may have more or less than this. It's not a good idea to press your baby to take a certain amount, or to try to restrict her intake if she seems to 'ask' for more, unless you have been given professional advice about it.

If your baby is only having an occasional bottle in place of a breastfeed, then the rule of thumb will help you assess the amount to prepare and offer. Divide the total amount your baby would need in a day by the number of feeds to get the amount of milk per feed. If your baby weighs 5 kilos, she would need something like 750 ml of formula a day if she were solely formula fed. If she feeds 10 times a day, she's likely to need about 75 ml at each feed. Make up 100 ml in case she wants more on that occasion. If your baby is heavier, say she weighs 8 kilos, for example, she will need about 1200 ml in 24 hours. If she only feeds six times a day, offer 200 ml at each feed.

Generally speaking, babies who are solely formula fed need to have the amount they are given increased as they grow (this is not the case with breastfed babies, whose intake tends to remain stable after the first three months, according to the research). This usually translates as larger amounts, given less often. A typical newborn may have eight or 10 small bottles of formula over the day and night; by the time she's aged three months, she might be having six or seven larger bottles instead.

Don't become anxious about the amount of formula taken and the frequency with which your baby feeds. Babies are individuals, and their personalities as well as their appetites play a role in how much they have, and when. Your best guide is your baby – her weight, health, development and behaviour are the factors you need to take into account.

COLD, WARM OR HOT?

You can use milk straight from the fridge if your baby is happy to take it. Newborns, and babies who have shown they don't like cold milk, can have their bottles warmed. Do this by standing the bottle in a jug of very hot water or in a bottle warmer. Heating in the microwave needs to be done with care – zap it for a few seconds only and tip up and down several times to eliminate the risks of hot spots that could scald. There's no evidence for the widespread belief that microwave heating destroys the nutrients in the milk.

Check the temperature very carefully when you heat the bottle. Do the drips on the wrist assessment (page 93) before giving it to your baby.

Don't assume your baby won't take cold milk, though. It's a lot less bother not to have to warm the milk – and if you are using the stand-in-a-jug warming method, it is less messy, too, with less risk of scalds. And, of course, your baby doesn't have to wait for her feed.

Note: Never put a bottle of formula milk or expressed breast milk back into the fridge if your baby has only taken some of it. You need to discard it.

HOW TO BOTTLEFEED YOUR BABY

Bottlefeeding is more than a way of getting milk into your baby. Just like breastfeeding, it is an important part of your nurturing, part of the relationship you and your baby are developing, and a major way for you and your baby to respond to each other.

When you bottlefeed, watch for feeding cues from your baby (page 55), and don't make her wait when you think she might be hungry. Your baby needs you to respond to her signals and doing so builds up her trust and confidence. You'll soon recognise when your baby needs feeding – she'll start moving her head, hands, arms and legs and become more agitated the longer she has to wait!

Hold your baby close to your body – as close as you can while still allowing room to hold the bottle comfortably. Avoid holding her flat on her back; that can mean the milk pours into her mouth, which makes it more difficult for her to co-ordinate sucking and swallowing, and to take breaks. A better position is semi-reclined.

Tempt your baby to open her mouth by moving the teat against her top lip, and, when her mouth is wide open, gently put the teat in so she can draw it back with her tongue and jaw. There is normally no need to poke, screw or force the teat in.

Tip the bottle up so the teat fills with milk. Your baby uses her tongue and lips to 'work' the teat and to control the flow of milk. Watch your baby and see if the teat appears comfortable – with so many styles available, one might be better than another (see page 91).

'Pace' the feed, by removing the teat when your baby's sucking slows down a little, and then replacing it, to give her a natural gap in her feeding, and to prevent over-feeding. Leaving the teat in can mean the milk is still dripping into her mouth, causing her to feed when her appetite would otherwise demand a break.

If your baby wriggles or fusses, this can mean she needs to change position for comfort, and she may want to get into an easier position to burp. There are lots of positions you can try.

- sitting her up
- lifting her so she can rest on your shoulder (put a cloth over your shoulder first)
- place her on her tummy over your lap.

Don't feel disappointed if she does not finish the bottle, or under any sort of pressure to get a certain amount of milk into your baby. Follow her appetite, and learn to accept that when she pushes the teat out with her tongue, or does not open to take the teat in again, or stops sucking strongly, she's probably had enough.

After the feed, it's normal for a baby to bring up a little milk. This is called 'possetting', and it's one of the reasons to keep a muslin cloth handy, ready for quick mopping up! Your baby will probably burp as well, to get rid of air she's taken in as she fed. For some babies wind seems to cause a problem and some discomfort. Your health visitor should be able to offer some advice you if your baby is distressed by wind.

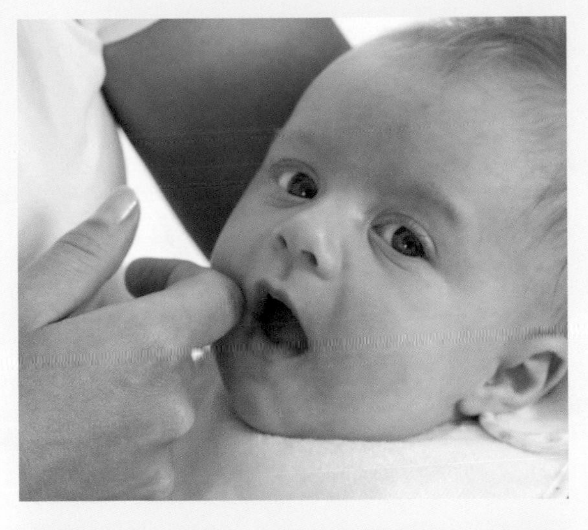

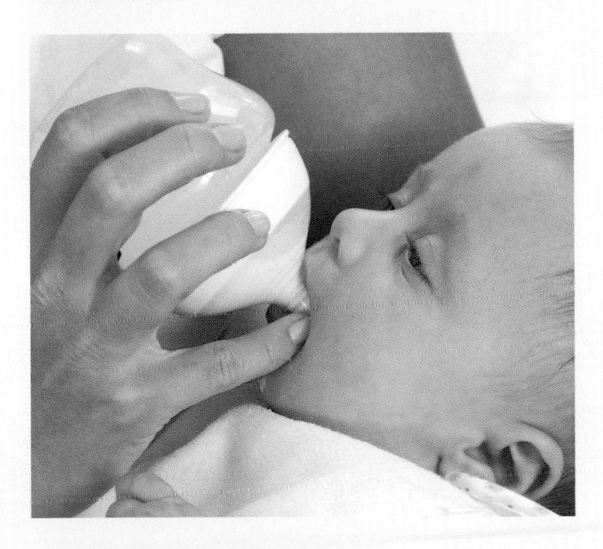

Feeding away from home

Formula feeding when you are not within reach of a kettle to boil water needs some pre-planning. Your will need:

- Clean, sterile bottle and teat, with a lid on to keep the teat clean.
- Measured amount of formula powder (you can buy special containers for this – make sure it is clean and sterile).
- Measured amount of hot water in a clean, sterile flask.
- When ready to use, pour the water from the flask into the bottle and add the powder as usual. Check the temperature of the water in case it remains too hot.
- If you take a ready-made-up bottle of milk with you, make sure you keep it cool (use a coolbag) and use it within a couple of hours.
- As an alternative, you can take a carton of ready-to-feed formula milk and a clean bottle.

Bonding with your baby

There are bound to be occasions when you hand your baby to someone else to feed, but it's important for your baby's social and emotional development and her developing attachment to you, that you are the main one – the one who does all or almost all the feeding, especially when your baby is very young. This is a way to make bottlefeeding more like breastfeeding, from your baby's point of view.

The apparent advantage of bottlefeeding – that anyone can do it – has the potential to be a big drawback. Babies who are regularly passed around for friends and relatives and other carers to 'have a turn' at feeding, and who may be swapped mid-feed to another bottle-holder, just aren't getting the experiences they need and thrive on.

Of course, letting this happen occasionally is not going to do your baby any harm. Some babies, however, make it clear they just haven't been comfortable, and react to the confusion (in their minds) and over-stimulation by being unsettled, or by 'switching off' and not feeding well. A bottle given by another carer – your

POSITIONS FOR BOTTLEFEEDING

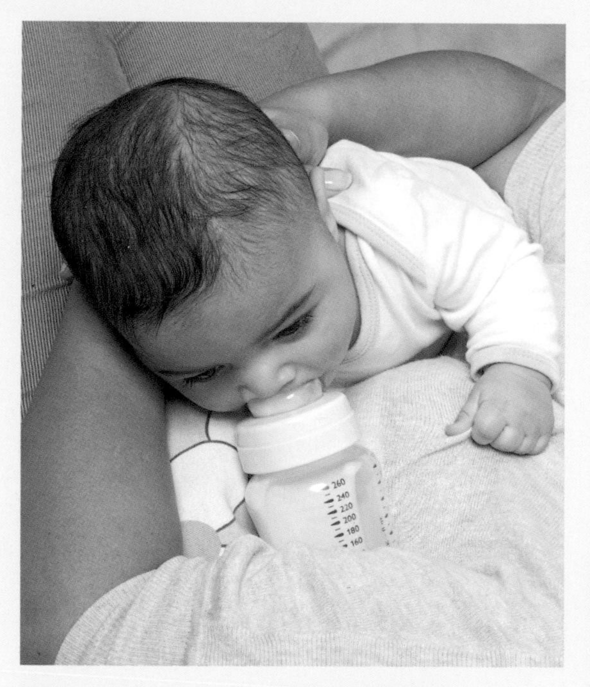

Bottle under arm to emulate breastfeeding

Cuddled in your arms

partner or a grandparent, perhaps – to help you take a break is fine, but it's not necessary for them to give a bottle in order to bond with your baby.

Explain to other people that they can't take the baby from you to feed her. You are not being selfish at all if you make it clear you want to be main person who gives your baby her bottle.

Enjoy being close when you're bottlefeeding and look at your baby when you feed, and have spontaneous little chats and interactions. Be responsive to her signals that she's had enough, that she wants a break from feeding, that she now wants to go back to it, that she wants to have a burp or change of position. Don't hold her on the same side every time; a breastfed baby has a different 'view' depending on whether she's on the right breast or the left breast, and you can emulate that by ringing the changes with your baby's position.

Facing mum

Skin-to-skin

Feelings about using formula

Most formula-fed babies started off by being breastfed – and many mothers who change to formula from breastfeeding wish they could have continued. Something like nine out of 10 mothers who stop breastfeeding before their baby is six weeks old say they would have liked to carry on but, for them, for whatever reason, breastfeeding did not work out well. So many formula-feeding mothers have, at the very least, mixed feelings about the whole thing.

If you have changed to formula feeding, there are a number of emotions you might experience some (or even all) of the time, especially at the beginning. They include:

- Relief at the end of the struggle to breastfeed (or to breastfeed completely if you are using formula in addition to breastfeeding).
- Sadness and disappointment, even grief, at the lost experience of breastfeeding.
- Gratitude that other people can give you a hand with this aspect of your baby's care.
- Guilt that this is not what you planned for your baby.
- A sense of freedom, because breastfeeding (or solely breastfeeding) felt like being 'tied'.
- Anger and frustration with yourself, with the people around you who did not help, or even with your baby.
- Defensiveness and touchiness with people who ask 'Oh, aren't you breastfeeding?'
- Sensitive and worried about what people might think of you using formula; even if no one says anything, you imagine what they might be thinking.
- Desperate for others to know you wanted to breastfeed.
- Embarrassed about formula feeding in front of other people.
- Worried about aspects of formula feeding, such as choice of brand, impact on your baby's health, how to do it safely.

A few mothers have negative feelings for a long time, even years, about their use of formula, or are defensive at what they frequently see as breastfeeding propaganda about the 'benefits' of breastfeeding or the 'risks' of formula feeding.

My own experience supporting mothers makes me believe very strongly that the emotional aspects and the mixed feelings are sometimes ignored – or if they're acknowledged, they're trivialized. Mothers who reveal their feelings to others hear that 'It makes no difference how a baby feeds – breast milk and formula are more or less the same now anyway' or 'Don't let people make you feel guilty; if you're happy formula feeding, then your baby's happy, too.'

Some strong feelings get expressed as dislike or scorn of the 'breastfeeding mafia' or 'nipple Nazis' or 'the Breastapo' (all epithets I've heard or seen in newspaper columns or online). These usually come from mothers whose own experience of breastfeeding has been dire and who report being made to feel guilty about switching to formula, or being pressured to continue with breastfeeding when it was clearly an unhappy experience.

Research done with formula-feeding mothers shows that these emotions appear genuine and

deep. Furthermore, concerns that there is little information about formula feeding, how to do it, and what formula to choose, add to feelings of isolation and confusion.

Formula-feeding mothers are not unique in feeling let down by a lack of information and support – it's questionable whether they are worse off than breastfeeding mothers, but just in a different way. Breastfeeding promotion over the past 20 or 30 years has not been matched with sufficient social acceptance and the enabling factors (good help when problems happen or flexible working, for example) we know are needed to make it successful. But there's also a lack of information to help mothers feel confident about formula feeding, so it's no surprise some women express huge irritation with 'the breastfeeding lobby'.

If you're formula feeding, and find breastfeeding promotion posters, leaflets or articles leave you feeling irritated and defensive, think about strategies that might help. You could try:

- Looking forward to the time when fewer and fewer people ask you about feeding.
- Explaining to people who do ask that it's a sensitive area for you – they'll soon change the subject.
- Not feeling guilty! While this is easier said than done, leave 'guilt' to people who have deliberately done something wrong; feeding your baby and doing your best for her doesn't deserve 'guilt'.
- Accept that you may feel sad and regretful (if you do) but see this as an inevitable part of parenting – no one gets it right for 20 years!
- Thinking about the statistics and feeling normal – the vast majority of babies (something like 98 per cent in the UK) have formula at some point, so you are doing nothing unusual at all.
- Enjoy feeding times – use them as a time for reveling in closeness and communication with your baby.
- Giving yourself a serious talking to if you're sensitive about people's remarks or looks – the chances are they are thinking nothing at all and may simply be stealing a glance at your lovely baby. No one has a right to judge you; anyone with a kind heart or who cares about you, wouldn't dream of having an opinion about a mother for not breastfeeding her baby.
- Thinking about maintaining some breastfeeding, alongside the formula feeding, if you wish (see 'mixed feeding' in chapter 7, pages 112–13).

All mothers need support and encouragement from the people around them, and if you are looking for information about formula, whether you're using it all the time or supplementing your breastfeeding with it, then you have a right to the information you need. Health visitors and midwives who use a phrase like 'I can't tell you about that as we have to promote breastfeeding', as apparently, and astonishingly, some of them do, are not doing their jobs properly. Ask to see someone who can tell you what you want to know – and complain about the one who refused to help you.

Special situations

Some babies are unable to feed from a bottle teat (or breast) because of mouth and jaw problems – a cleft lip and/or cleft palate, perhaps, or other difficulty. Sick or pre-term babies may have difficulty co-ordinating sucking, swallowing and breathing. Babies with Down's syndrome may have the same issues.

Special teats and feeding bottles (like the Haberman feeder, now called the Special Needs feeder) can address these problems. If your baby is in this sort of situation, the paediatric team should be aware of your options and offer information and advice. They should also be able to let you know where you can get your supplies of bottles and teats, and how to use them effectively.

Twins and triplets

It's hard (but not impossible) to bottlefeed twins at the same time. One way is to place your babies on a supportive pillow and feed them face-to-face with a bottle in each of your hands.

Some parents take the chance to feed their babies one at a time, and that way each baby gets a good close-up cuddle and some individual attention from you as well. This is fine if one baby is prepared to wait. It is not so good if you're alone and both babies are hungry and fussing. If you and your partner share feeds, try to even things out so each baby gets time with both of you.

Fairly obviously, triplets can't be fed by one person at one time – not enough hands!

Using expressed breast milk

You may prefer to or need to feed your baby breast milk from a bottle for a number of reasons including:

- Your baby can't feed directly from the breast for some reason, or does not feed sufficiently well (sucking problems, usually, or perhaps she is small, sick or pre-term).
- You are not around; perhaps you're having a break, a rest or a night off!
- You work away from the home.
- You simply prefer to feed with a bottle.
- You have very sore, cracked or damaged nipples and they may need a break to heal.

Expressing is a useful skill, and it's often very handy to have this option but giving expressed milk in a bottle 'to give you a break' is not always the kind favour it sounds! A bottle of expressed milk creates a longer gap between breastfeeds, which means your breasts feel uncomfortably full in the short term, and your milk supply will be reduced in the medium or long term.

If you decide to introduce bottles of expressed milk, read the information on mixed feeding in chapter 7 (pages 112–13), so you have the details you need to make a choice.

There are situations where you might express milk and not feed it to your baby. If you are taking medication that's incompatible with breastfeeding, for example, and breastfeeding is suspended you can express in order to maintain the production line. You would discard the milk (this is known as 'pump and dump'). Occasionally, gentle hand expressing may help with a blocked duct or mastitis (see page 81), but in this case your baby can have the milk, or you can freeze it for later use.

Expressing your milk

You can express by hand, or with a pump. Hand pumps are cheaper than electric ones, but slightly harder work to use. Hand expressing with no pump is the cheapest option of all and

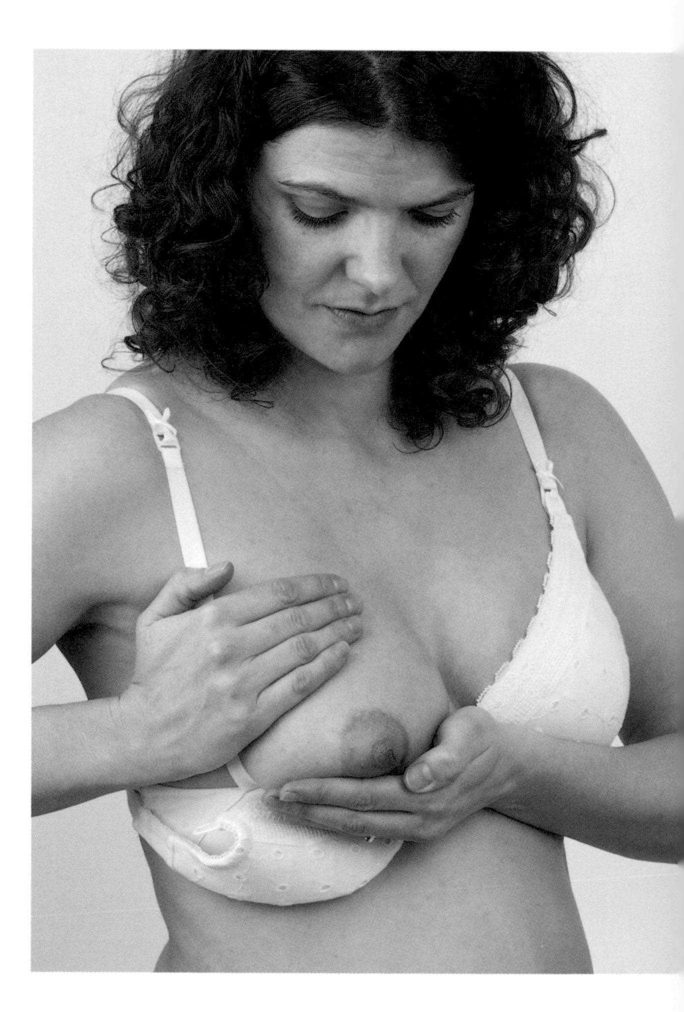

some women get good results, but it can be hard work if you are doing it several times a day.

By hand

1. Relax, and sit or stand comfortably, with a sterilised bowl in front of you on the table, at a height to catch the milk.
2. Gently support your breast with one hand. With the other, stroke the breast from the top towards the nipple (see photograph, left).
3. Place the fingers and thumb of the 'stroking hand' about 2 cm away from the end of your nipple, and squeeze them gently together. The idea is to put pressure on the milk reservoirs – you may need to experiment. Keep squeezing, and rolling a little towards the nipple. Move around, so you press on different reservoirs. It's normal to get drips, and then spurts, as you activate your let-down reflex (see page 54).
4. Swap breasts when your spurts become drips; some women find it's worthwhile swapping back again to give each breast two expressions.

Hand or electric pump?

If you use a pump, the instructions that go with the model you have chosen will be provided. Some women find they're successful with one type and not with others. If you buy one and it doesn't work for you, take it back for a refund.

All pumps have a flange which goes over your nipple and areola, and they collect your milk in a bottle-shaped container at the same time as you pump.

There's some evidence that electric pumps, which allow both breasts to be pumped at once because they have a container and tubing for each breast, stimulate the breasts more effectively and can save time. Hiring a large electric pump is only worthwhile, however, if you plan to use it for a month or so. If you think you might express over a longer period, then buying your own will work out cheaper. Always sterilise the parts of the pump that come into contact with your milk between uses.

How much?

If your baby is in special care, you'll be expressing to prime and then maintain a milk supply for when your baby is able to feed directly from you (see page 52). Quantity is not crucial – the more the better!

If you're expressing for an older baby at home, use the rule-of-thumb described on pages 96–7 to work out how much your baby is likely to need, until you get to know from experience how much your baby takes at a feed.

Storing breast milk

Store your expressed milk in the fridge (it's safe for up to five days – a lot longer than formula) or in the freezer (safe for six months). You can buy specially made bags to store your expressed breast milk; don't use ordinary ones, which can split and which may not be safe for food use. Defrost in the fridge for 12 hours, and throw away any unused milk after a feed.

CHAPTER 7

Patterns in baby feeding

Once the newborn stage has passed, you – and your baby – will become aware that different needs, demands and expectations have to be met. You may want to think about how you can bring about changes to the patterns of your days and nights. Is there a case for working out a timetable for care, or a feeding schedule, or does this seem too inflexible for you? Do you want to 'lead' your baby or 'be led by' him? Or do you aim for a compromise between the two?

You will want to consider for how long you accept unpredictability. If your baby hasn't 'settled', you'll need to find the ways that will soothe him and keep him happier. If you decide to choose 'combination' or 'mixed' feeding, which means your baby breastfeeds (or has expressed breast milk) as well as having formula milk, handle will you meet the issues that may arise.

There are no answers that all parents agree on, but what we know of how babies develop supports the choice to continue responsive, child-centred care throughout infancy and babyhood. Such an approach doesn't have to mean exhausted, sleepless nights or a whining, demanding toddler. Night times can be made easier and the child whose needs are acknowledged and met is likely to grow up more confident and with less need to whine.

Baby-led feeding

The lack of routine and pattern in a young baby's life can be the most worrying and exhausting thing for new mothers. Personal accounts of how heavy this weighs on a mother's energy levels, of how it impacts on her view of herself as a capable, in-control person, have led to a popular genre of writing known as 'mummy lit'. In many of these books, the fatigue and lack of confidence felt by new mothers are graphically described. Internet forums echo these same feelings. The desire to 'fix' the dependency of a new baby, to marshal it so it becomes manageable, lies behind the popularity of many other books, those that set out instructions on what you and your baby should be doing at all times of the day.

Accepting your baby's needs

There's plenty of evidence to show that babies flourish best when their needs are accepted, and when the people who love them respond to them quickly and sensitively. (Baby-led breastfeeding ensures an adequate milk supply, too.) Usually, this means frequent feeding day and night, which ties in with what we know about babies' social and cognitive development, and the way their metabolism digests breast milk quickly and efficiently.

The cluster-feeding that's common in small babies – short feeds close together punctuated by short naps, still held in your arms – seems particularly likely to happen in the evening, but can also happen at other times. And there will also be times when a baby changes his pattern and wants to be fed more often than before. This situation is sometimes explained by the words 'growth spurt', but it may not be linked with a physical need to grow. Instead, it could be a reflection of an emotional need to stay close to you, and to have some intense, comforting interaction with you.

It is easier to accept these needs – just as it is easier to accept night waking than to try to 'train' it out of a young baby. While your baby is very young, you need to be patient with yourself and your baby. If you respond to your baby's unpredictable, needy urgency for care and attention, your baby will grow in confidence and trust, which allows him to be less dependent as he grows. But it is also true that you need support and tender loving care as well. You need to permit the people who love you to rally round and take over any other tasks that need doing.

There are many effective ways to nudge your baby towards a compromise – keeping him comforted and well-fed while you have a routine and a regular shape to your day – and they can start at any age, though expecting results with a newborn is asking a bit too much. Days and nights change very quickly when your baby is young and getting used to the world. Lots of parents choose to go down this route, because caring for a baby is not the only thing they have to do, especially as the weeks go by and they get back to some of their 'old' life. The only wrong way to fit your baby's needs in with your life is to impose a routine on him without sufficient consideration for his needs.

Some sort of routine

Here are some suggestions you can try when your baby is a little older – maybe from a few weeks onwards:

- Create a bedtime routine, which includes bathing your baby at roughly the same time each evening. Babies usually enjoy a bath, and it doesn't have to be the mother who does it. Follow the bath with a quiet feed to help wind your baby down for the evening.
- Always aim to get yourself up at the same time each day, have breakfast and get dressed. Feed your baby even if he hasn't asked for it.
- If you need to go out somewhere, feed your baby before you go, so you reduce the chance of your baby being hungry when you are in transit (this will not always work!).
- 'Wear' your baby in a sling or baby carrier (you can do this from birth, of course). You need to experiment with different ways of wrapping one, or even trying different types if you can borrow a few before buying, to get one that feels comfortable for you. A sling or carrier will make breastfeeding on the move a lot easier and if your baby needs soothing after a feed in order to settle, the physical closeness of being tucked up next to your body often does the job.
- Gently wake your baby up if he dozes mid-feed and encourage him to feed more, so you can end the feed and get on with something else. There is absolutely no problem doing this and most mothers do it without even thinking about it after a while, sensing when their baby is not quite finished, and tickling his cheek or his hands, or taking the bottle or breast out of his mouth, to perk him up.
- Get out of the house at least once a day. There are many social activities and groups for mums and babies you could join. While you might need to be quite brave to do this, especially if you're shy, it is worth it to meet other parents (who may feel just as disorganised as you do). Regular dates for different events give your week a structure, which helps.
- If you're bottlefeeding, create a routine for cleaning and sterilising (see page 94).

Once your baby is having solid foods regularly, you are likely to have breakfast, lunch and tea/dinner plus a mid-morning and mid-afternoon snack together, at fairly predictable times. This in itself gives a structure to the day, without any hard work.

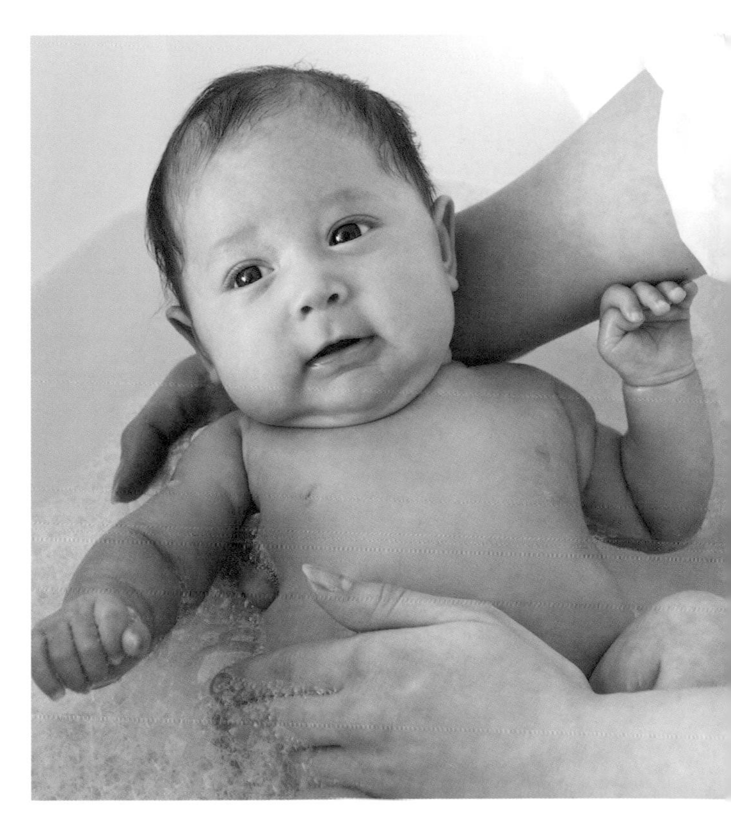

Mixed feeding

Babies who are breastfed without anything else until they're ready for solid foods – usually about the middle of the first year (see page 122) – enjoy the best health in the long term. Breast milk supplies all the baby needs by way of food and drink until that time, and when it's going well, healthy babies don't need water, or 'top ups' of formula milk, or vitamins or any supplementary foods. Formula is the only safe alternative to breast milk for a baby under the age of six months.

But what if breastfeeding isn't going well? Or if you want to introduce formula milk alongside breastfeeding? Or if you are told your baby needs to have a formula feed instead of a breastfeed, which would mean he would miss out an entire breastfeed, or a top up of formula after a breastfeed?

Deciding to offer some formula milk is a more complicated decision than you might assume, as formula almost always has some effect on your breastfeeding.

Because the breast milk supply is driven by frequent, effective milk removal, formula has an impact on the supply-and-demand process. Formula takes longer than breast milk to digest, so even a small amount can lengthen the gaps between breastfeeds, and long gaps suppress

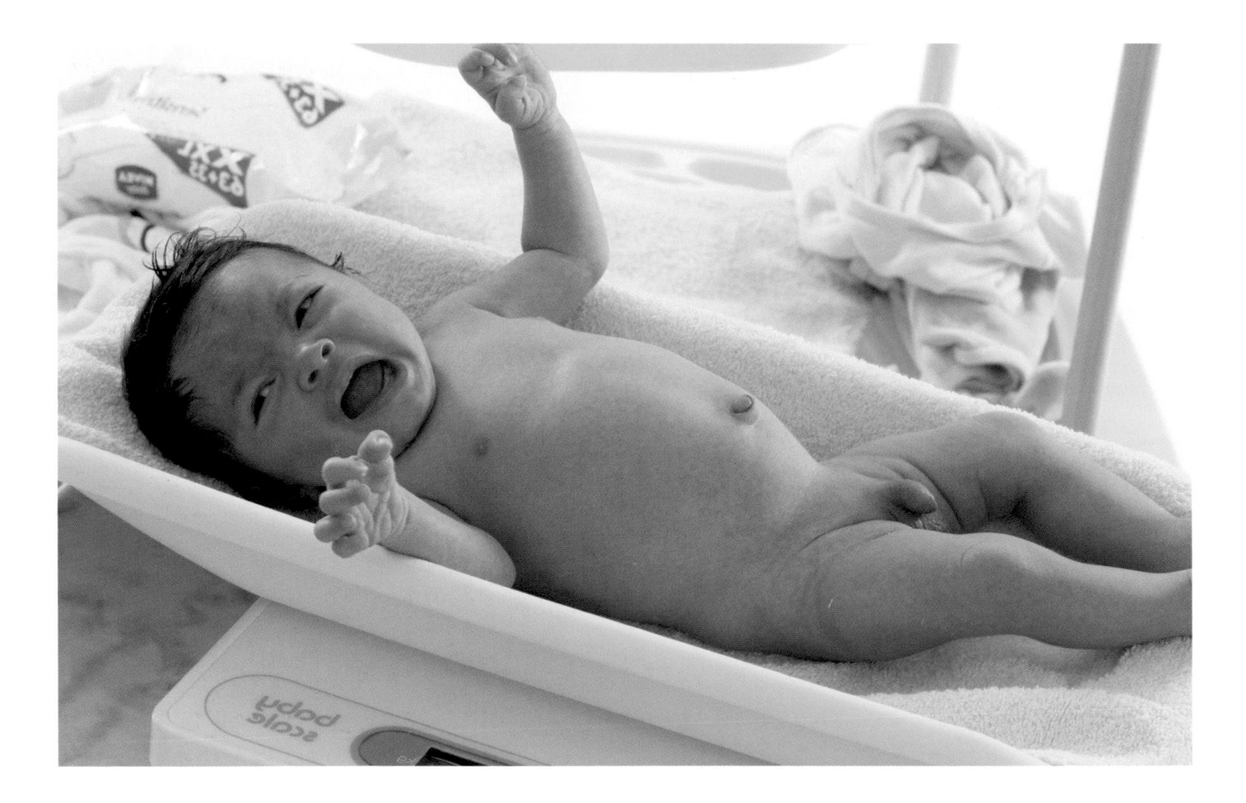

production. This means that 'mixed feeding' can become 'mostly formula feeding' and then 'solely formula feeding', because as breastfeeding lessens, your baby has to be fed somehow (clearly) and formula takes its place. The longer you breastfeed without formula, the more robust your breast milk supply becomes, and the less likely it is to dwindle away after the introduction of formula. The smaller the amount of formula, the less impact it has, too.

The breastfeeding 'production line' needs round-the-clock, frequent stimulation to get underway, and early introduction of formula can undermine this. While it's possible to go back to full breastfeeding, or maintain some breastfeeding, it can be a challenge.

Findings of the UK Infant Feeding Survey show that breastfed babies who have had some formula in the first week are much more likely to be fully formula fed by the age of two weeks than babies who have had none. Some people claim this is partly to do with so-called nipple confusion – the introduction of the bottle teat has caused a baby to forget how to suck from the breast. I am pretty certain this is not the case – there's no real evidence that a baby's instinct to suck from the breast can disappear, and plenty of evidence that one is able to manage both breast and bottle – but if the breast is unproductive or unrewarding, the baby can reject it.

So for mixed feeding to 'work', your baby should only have formula in the early days if it is medically necessary (as it sometimes is), and with careful measures to make sure your breastfeeding, and your comfort, are protected (that means expressing to avoid gaps between milk removal – see page 106).

If you plan to use formula alongside breastfeeding, it's best to wait; as we've seen, mixed feeding stops being mixed if you start too soon. Instead, try to introduce formula only once your breastfeeding is well established, to a baby who's healthy and gaining weight, and who's already a few months old. That way your milk supply is more likely to remain reliable.

When is mixed feeding needed?

- If the baby can't get what he needs from breast milk in order to thrive, formula is a necessary addition to breastfeeding. Sometimes, breastfeeding gets off to a difficult start, and formula is given, usually only in the short term, to ensure the baby is well-fed, hydrated and has the energy to breastfeed more effectively.
  However, formula in these circumstances is only needed if you are not able to, or choose not to, supplement or top up with your own expressed breast milk, which your baby can have by bottle, spoon, cup or syringe. A further alternative is donor milk (see page 75).
- If you or your healthcare professional is concerned about your baby's weight or his satisfaction on breast milk alone, formula might be advised as a 'top up'.
  The trouble with topping up is that it doesn't address the underlying problem, if there is one, and if there isn't one, it can create one where none existed. If your baby is thought to need more calories, then you have them already – in your breasts. If you and your baby needs help to make feeding more effective, then someone knowledgeable and supportive such as a breastfeeding counsellor can observe you feeding and suggest changes in positioning, if needed.

Usually, though, it's a question of breastfeeding more often, and using both breasts (at least) each time – that has the happy effect of boosting your supply and boosting your baby's intake.

- If you plan to be away from your baby, and know he is likely to need a feed when you're not there, his caregiver/babysitter needs to know how to prepare a bottle for him.
  You can express in advance, or if you choose not to do this, your baby will need formula. You may need to express for comfort while you're away (see breastfeeding and working, page 32, for more details). See the 'rule-of -thumb' guidance (page 966) for assessing the quantity of formula your baby is likely to need.
- In an attempt to help a baby sleep earlier in the evening and to stay asleep for longer, formula is sometimes given.
  The assumption here is that formula takes longer to digest, so a large volume of formula milk may 'fill the baby up' more effectively than a breastfeed. The trouble is, there's no guarantee this works, and the studies that have been done indicate that parents get more sleep if their baby is fully breastfed. This is probably because while formula can sometimes settle a baby and encourage a longer continuous sleep, the feed itself takes time to prepare and give to the baby. Result? The adults(s) may actually be awake for longer. The breastfed baby often feeds at night with minimal disturbance to his mother (or her still-sleeping partner) and obviously with no preparation.
- To 'give mum a break' – and that can be a welcome offer if she can catch up on sleep.
  However, it's less welcome when formula is given so the bottle-wielding adult can chill on the sofa in front of the TV while the mother gets on with the ironing! This is another situation where expressed breast milk can be an alternative, but skipping breastfeeds is not a great favour to you if you are uncomfortable as a result, or if your supply is affected.

All this sounds as if any possible positive of additional formula is wiped out by a negative – and that there's nothing to be said for mixed feeding. Not true. There are circumstances when using formula might be an essential back up to an individual mother. A mother who feels overwhelmed by a baby who needs a great deal of attention might find having a break while someone gives a bottle of formula gives her the resilience she needs and she copes better overall. Just occasionally, breastfeeding might need to be suspended for a short while: incompatible medication, hospital treatment or some other emergency might mean formula for that time (while expressing, if possible, to maintain the milk supply). Or a 'convenience bottle' given by a partner could help make an evening routine more manageable.

It's not true that giving formula 'wipes out all the benefit of breastfeeding'. The research indicates a spectrum – breastfeeding retains its antibodies and protective qualities whether or not formula is given, and babies only partially breastfed are still less likely to pick up infections or need medical treatment than babies who are fully formula fed. Unsurprisingly, predominant breastfeeding appears to be better than partial breastfeeding, and partial breastfeeding appears to be better than predominant formula feeding.

As ever, health and nutrition are not the only factors that play a part in decisions, and mixed feeding can be an informed, and an appropriate, choice for you and your baby.

HOW LONG TO BREASTFEED OR BOTTLEFEED?

There is no upper age limit for breastfeeding or bottlefeeding. However, if your child is still using a bottle for all his drinks beyond the age of about one, then think about swapping at least some of these for a cup. This is to protect his teeth and his nutrition. The 'all day' bottle that toddlers sometimes get very attached to, hanging on to it and taking a swig off and on, is not good for dental health (unless it's water in the bottle). The other aspect is that when milk is always in the bottle, it can take the place of other foods and tastes.

Toddlers find an evening bottle of milk very comforting and part of their settling-down ritual – but dentists don't like it, as the teeth become bathed in milk last thing in the evening. If your toddler's still loathe to give it up, then clean his teeth before bed, and put water in his bottle after that (you might have to do this gradually, diluting the post-teeth-cleaning bottle very slightly more, over time).

Breastfeeding babies beyond infancy is something that gets the Western media in a frenzy every so often – there is a fascination with the question of 'how old is too old?' and commentators are free with their outrage, shock and judgements. This is entirely culture-led of course, as breastfeeding older toddlers and children is not especially unusual in some societies. Researchers who have asked mothers in the West what they actually do, find that true 'child-led weaning' starts at about age two to three, and the whole process takes a few years to complete. It's unusual for a four, five or six year old to still breastfeed, and those that do, may be having no more than the very occasional suckle by the end of their time as 'breastfeeders', so working out exactly when they stopped is difficult. It seems that beyond this age, the ability to suckle disappears.

There's no evidence that mothers 'make' their children continue breastfeeding or that there is any harm, physically or emotionally, in what has become known as 'natural term breastfeeding' (a phrase used instead of 'extended breastfeeding' among mothers who breastfeed beyond a year or so). Weaning an older baby or toddler (or child) is beyond the scope of this book, and if you decide to take the initiative and speed things up, then that's fine, too, of course.

How feeding differs over time

A number of changes take place as your baby gets older and his development shapes his behaviour. You might see signs of them, or some signs of them, from about three months on.

If you are breastfeeding

- Some feeds get shorter, as your baby starts to become more interested in his surroundings and more distractable. He feeds efficiently, and takes what he needs in a shorter time.
  There is no need to try to force him to stay on for longer, or to assume he's not getting what he needs to grow and stay healthy – if he's healthy and thriving, you can rely on him to take what he needs. When he stops, he may want to play or chat.
- The feed before your baby's longest sleep remains a longer one.
  Enjoy this snuggly togetherness as your baby calms and quietens after a busy day.
- Your baby looks to the breast for comfort and nuzzles you when he's upset to indicate he'd like a breastfeed, not just when he's hungry or thirsty.
  Breastfeeding can be a good comforter when your baby has the normal knocks and bumps

that come with crawling or when he is tired or upset. If you've spent time away from him, even a couple of hours, he may well show you his need to 'reconnect' by relishing a breastfeed. A breastfeed makes lots of things 'all right'!

If you are bottlefeeding

- Your baby starts to want to hold the bottle, or place his hands on it; it's fine to let him do this.
  This is normal development, and many babies will be capable of holding and drinking from their own bottle from about nine or ten months on. It's good to continue to hold your baby for some bottlefeeds, though. Don't leave your baby alone with his feeding bottle.
- Your baby shows signs of excitement, even joy, when he sees you preparing a bottle for him, showing you that his pleasure in feeding time is more than just a matter of satisfying his hunger.
  This might happen from just a few weeks old.

Sleep regression

Whether you breastfeed or bottlefeed, your baby starts to wake up more often during the night, and needs help to get back to sleep again. This so-called sleep regression often happens at around three or four months, but it can happen at any time. It is often associated with a developmental leap, or teething (see page 125), or a change in surroundings or routine, or the after effects of a mild illness. It's as if your baby needs extra reassurance at these times because of discomfort or confusion, or just needs you more for some reason. I am not convinced by explanations related to a baby's sleep cycles changing at this age, but who knows ... the fact is that babies who used to sleep for several hours at a time stop doing so, and it's so common, it must be normal! The regression may last a week or two or a little more. It's often heard that night waking is a sign of increasing hunger that milk alone cannot satisfy and it's therefore a sign to wean on to solid foods. This is unlikely as we will see in chapter 8.

Ride the storm and respond to your baby with whatever comfort he needs, including a breast- or bottlefeed. Just as when he was younger, he's waking and crying from genuine need, and not to manipulate you.

Co-sleeping

The majority of babies in the world don't sleep alone, and research by baby sleep expert Professor Helen Ball shows the majority of UK babies sleep with their parents some of the time – it's very normal parental care. Some parents choose to co-sleep routinely; others bring their baby into bed for part of the night, often to try to help them settle and sleep better, and to make feeding easier.

There are concerns about safety. Adult beds are not designed or made with the safety and wellbeing of babies in mind, so you may need to put some thought into making your bed a safe as well as a comforting place for your baby. The main concerns are that your baby should not become too hot, and that you should be able to remain aware of his presence at all times. In addition, co-sleeping should not expose your baby to the risks of cigarettes, and the bed itself should not be able to trap your baby's limbs or head between mattress and wall or bed frame. All of these aspects have been linked with the risk of death, including sudden infant death syndrome.

Happily, there has been a large amount of research into what makes co-sleeping safe, and following evidence-based guidance means your baby is at no greater risk in bed with you, than he is in a cot. Leaflets are available from UNICEF which give detailed advice on ensuring your baby is safe when he sleeps with you. The basics to remember are:

- Never co-sleep on a sofa or an armchair.
- Check your bed and your mattress to make sure there is no way your baby could become trapped, or fall out; your mattress should be firm with no sagging.
- Don't co-sleep if you or your partner smoke.
- Don't co-sleep if you are affected by drugs or alcohol.
- Don't leave your baby alone in your bed.
- Your baby should not overheat – keep his nightwear light, make sure covers can't go over his head, and that he cannot go under the pillow or press his face into the pillow.

UNICEF reports that research shows that breastfeeding mothers naturally form a 'nest' around their baby with their body which protects the baby and stops him moving up and down the bed. If you are not breastfeeding, UNICEF says the safest place for your baby to sleep is in a bed in your room.

BABIES AND NIGHT TIMES

Babies are designed to wake and feed many times during the night while adults prize a largely unbroken night. It's assumed that today's parents want a baby whose night-time habits allow for this, if not in the first weeks, then certainly within the first months.

There are plenty of how-to books, and 'sleep specialists' and 'sleep clinics' offering to help you and your baby achieve several hours of sleep. Their tactics always involve some degree of ignoring your baby's expressed desires, in the hope that he'll learn not to express them.

The strictest of these techniques demand you ignore these desires completely, by only feeding, cuddling and even interacting, with your baby at scheduled times. Less harsh programmes allow for some flexibility, but still try to reduce unpredictability and waking by fobbing the baby off with patting and shushing, and leaving him unfed, uncuddled and ignored. All this has been described by a New Yorker I know who works with new mothers as 'beating the baby's normal physiology into submission' and it's not doing a lot of good to the baby's normal emotional and social development, either.

It is easier, and kinder, to change your own expectations of what makes a good night's rest than to change your baby's normal and developmentally appropriate need to wake, feed and fall asleep again…and then wake and feed again later, and again, and sometimes again. Paradoxically, on-and-off waking and feeding is something that becomes easier if you accept it and accommodate it. This might mean co-sleeping (see opposite). It certainly means sleeping in the same room, close to your baby for at least the first six months. It means keeping night feeds low key and not changing nappies unless it's absolutely necessary (major leakages or a sore bottom). While breastfeeding is easier than bottlefeeding at night, because of the nil preparation and the way you can do it without fully waking up yourself (in time), it's also possible to make bottlefeeding less disturbing. Make up a bottle before bed and store it in a coolbag (as you would when you're out and about, page 99) or pour ready-to-feed formula into a clean bottle.

Sleep training a young baby teaches a pre-verbal, non-reasoning infant that even when he is distressed or lonely, or hungry or thirsty, no one will put things right. After a time, the baby stops crying for attention at night as a result.

There is a plausible, evolution-based explanation for this 'learned' silence: crying is a survival mechanism but a baby stops crying when no one arrives to 'rescue' him because it is safer for a helpless infant to be quiet when left alone (he is less likely to attract a wild animal).

So leaving a baby to cry it out, or whatever variation on ignoring is on offer, may work but what has a baby actually learned?

Note: Sleep training a pre-schooler is a different matter as you can use consistency and calm with a child who can talk and reason.

CHAPTER 8

Adding other foods and drinks

Guidance to parents and healthcare and children's services professionals in the UK and majority of the world, echoes the World Health Organisation's recommendation that exclusive breastfeeding – breastfeeding without other foods and drinks – provides the best nutrition for babies until the age of six months, and that breast milk or formula milk meets the nutritional requirements of most healthy babies for the first six months of life.

However, this does not mean that every individual baby will want to adhere to this guideline. Some babies will start to show signs of being ready for other foods before, and some after, this age. This chapter shows how you can respond sensitively to your baby's needs and support an enjoyable weaning stage that eases the transition to a healthy toddler diet.

When to start

Breastfeeding or formula feeding, or a mix of the two, will be all your baby needs for several months. After that, your baby will benefit from a wider range of tastes, textures, and nutrients. At first, other foods will be an addition to her milk, and then as time goes on, these other foods will become the main part of her diet. Adding food is sometimes known as 'weaning', which is confusing, because 'weaning' also means 'stopping breastfeeding' or 'stopping bottlefeeding' altogether.

Foods other than milk are usually known as 'solids', 'solid foods' or sometimes 'complementary foods', and the right time for your baby to have them is far from precise. Eating other foods is a stage of development, rather than an event on the calendar; babies are no more ready for solids all at the same age any more than they are all ready for walking at the same age.

The most widely adopted guidance issued by government health departments and healthcare and children's services comes from the World Health Organisation, whose systematic review of the evidence was published in 2001 and then affirmed once more in 2009.

The review concluded that a public health programme based on recommending exclusive breastfeeding – breastfeeding without other foods and drinks – for six months supports health and nutrition, and babies who breastfeed in this way show no disadvantages in terms of growth or development. The recommendation applies to all settings, in developed and developing countries, because the evidence assessed came from a wide range of studies, using different types of populations.

As a piece of public health guidance, the WHO's recommendation is sound, but it is not a set of instructions to individual parents of

First solids can be anything but solid – many parents start their babies with fruit or vegetable purées which can be messy. Put a big bib or cloth around the baby's neck, and protect the floor with a waterproof sheet.

individual babies – and that's where misunderstanding can creep in. Some parents think they must wean on a certain day, and no earlier or later, and sometimes become anxious if their baby seems uncooperative. It's also the case that there's not much research into when formula- or mixed-fed babies start to need solids, at least not enough to make a similar very age-specific policy (though we do know that before 17 weeks is 'too early' for most babies; see page 129). Some countries make no distinction in their guidance – it's six months for all babies, however they are fed. Others say four months for formula- or mixed-fed babies, and six months for those who are breastfed. Not all experts agree that six months is the 'right' public health message for all babies, and there is an on-going dialogue in the academic journals about this.

When it comes to observing what happens in the real world, it's clear babies don't all become ready for solid food at the same age (no surprises there). However, the signs babies are 'ready' are not always well understood; sometimes, babies are given solids as a response to waking more in the night, or because they seem fractious and fussy. Hunger for solids is probably not the reason for these behaviours, however.

What we can say is that there appears to be a span of a couple of months or so, starting around the middle of the first year, when babies who are given the chance to handle foods for themselves, indicate readiness by showing interest. They also have developed some ability in eating, chewing and swallowing around this time. Some babies seem ready and able a bit before six months, and some don't show any signs at all until a little after.

It may be that public health guidance changes as more research becomes available, but individual babies will always vary in how quickly and readily they wean from a milk-only diet.

Is my baby ready for other foods?

As well as discounting exact age, not sleeping or looking at other people eating are not necessarily signs your baby is ready. Babies wake up at night for many reasons, including hunger and thirst, and it's fine to give your baby a breast- or bottlefeed if this is what calms and settles her. There's no evidence that the small amount of solid foods babies have when they first start on them makes any difference to sleeping patterns in general. You may observe a difference in your baby, but it would be difficult to prove it was the solids that caused it.

If your baby looks at other people eating, this is a sign of her being sociable and interested in the world around her. It makes no more sense to start giving your baby other foods because she watches you eat than it would to assume she's ready for driving lessons because she reaches out towards the steering wheel when she sees you driving.

The health evidence is that some time around the middle of the first year babies start to need more iron than is available to them in breast milk, and more calories than they can get even if they breast- or formula feed a lot. Note the word 'start'; no baby wakes up on any day, at four, six or eight months, desperate for more iron, or indeed anything else. You can easily meet this gradually increasing need by making other foods available to your baby at about six months.

Be led by your baby's appetite when deciding on quantity and frequency, and by your knowledge of what makes a healthy, varied diet. There's no rush to have a huge repertoire of different foods or to have regular meal-sized quantities. In fact, building up pressure on either of these points can lead to fussiness and refusal. Meals and eating should be enjoyable and a bit of a social occasion, too.

Nature gives us some pretty clear hints on why 'about six months' is a good guide for most babies when you observe a baby's development at this time:

- An important factor is that the first teeth start appearing around six months so babies are able to develop a good chewing motion. They also will have lost the young baby's tongue-thrust reflex that tends to push food out. For this reason when you feed a young baby you need to use a spoon to tip the food in, over the tongue (and of course the food has to be smooth and lump-free).
- A second factor is that babies of this age are capable of holding things purposefully and hanging on to them, and they have enough hand-eye co-ordination to bring an object (like a piece of food) to their mouths.
- Finally, with a bit of support at first, they can sit up comfortably.

SPOON-FED OR BABY-LED WEANING?

Over the past couple of generations, the usual way to introduce solid foods has been to make a purée of fruit or vegetables, or to use a proprietary brand of baby cereal or rice, often mixed with formula milk, and give this to a baby, starting with tiny amounts, off a spoon. Typically, a baby might have two or three teaspoonsful once a day, building up to twice, and then three times a day, with an extra spoonful or two each time. The amounts increase in quantity as your baby grows, but the food is limited to bland tastes, and smooth textures for the first weeks. Small jars of ready-prepared foods are also available, and the age guidance on the label helps you decide when to offer them. Foods that include lumps and chunks are usually labelled for babies over nine months.

If you decide to choose spoon-feeding, then go at your baby's pace. Observing her reactions will help you decide how fast to go; your baby may spit some tastes out, hold the food in her mouth without swallowing, or push the spoon away. Or she might show by her keenness to open her mouth that's she's enjoying the experience and ready for more.

If it helps you to have a plan – and some mothers gain confidence with a fairly detailed 'weaning calendar' that gives times, dates, quantities and recipes – your health visitor will

have a 'weaning sheet' she can give you. All the baby food manufacturers have them, too, but of course they're trying to sell you their own branded products, so read them with that knowledge in mind.

The other approach is to leave a lot of the decision-making about what to eat and how much of it to your baby. Sometimes called 'self-feeding', or 'baby-led weaning', this approach to weaning puts your child in control, and means you have far less need to make (or buy) any special baby food. You enable your baby to learn about taste, texture and eating by giving her suitable pieces of food – known as 'finger foods' – she can safely and enjoyably eat, and letting her have fun with them.

One way of starting this when she's about six months old is to share some of your food with your baby, and see what she does with it. Try with a banana, or a piece of bread, or a cooked carrot – and go on from there. Give your baby suitably sliced, cut or spooned-out portions of what you would eat yourself, and let her pick it up and eat what she manages.

It's certainly messy, at least at first, and if you're worried about food being handled and smeared around, then...well, you might have to put those concerns aside for a while. Spaghetti bolognese is probably not the dish to offer if you're somewhere a great deal of mess is going to matter, but it's a great experience when you're at home with a protective covering on the floor and an open

acceptance of food being played with as well as eaten (some of it, that is).

If your baby is six months or older and has no apparent allergies or food sensitivities, she can have any food, as long as it is not over-salty or over-spiced, or highly sweetened, and as long as it's unlikely to break off in her mouth and cause a choking hazard (a slice of apple, for example, is not a good thing for a new self-feeder). Babies do splutter sometimes when self-feeding – they're gagging, rather than choking, using their tongue to bring a large lump to the front of the mouth again. An infant resuscitation session is a good idea whether you intend weaning this way or not. This will teach you to distinguish between gagging and choking and what to do about the former (nothing except observe) and the latter, which could be a life-threatening situation. See page 129–131 for ideas on what makes good baby-led weaning foods.

Equipment needs

The only thing that's really useful for this stage of feeding is a high chair – and even that's not essential all the time, as babies can sit on laps quite comfortably. A fold-away chair is good for small kitchens and one with a removable tray and an adjustable-height seat means you can use it at the table when your baby gets a bit older.

You don't need a special baby food processor – it's no more useful than a regular one. Mashing with a fork or fine chopping will make any food manageable for a baby, and simple slicing to make sticks is all you will need if you decide to give your baby finger foods. If you want to make smooth-textured purées or soups for your baby, a normal food processor will be fine.

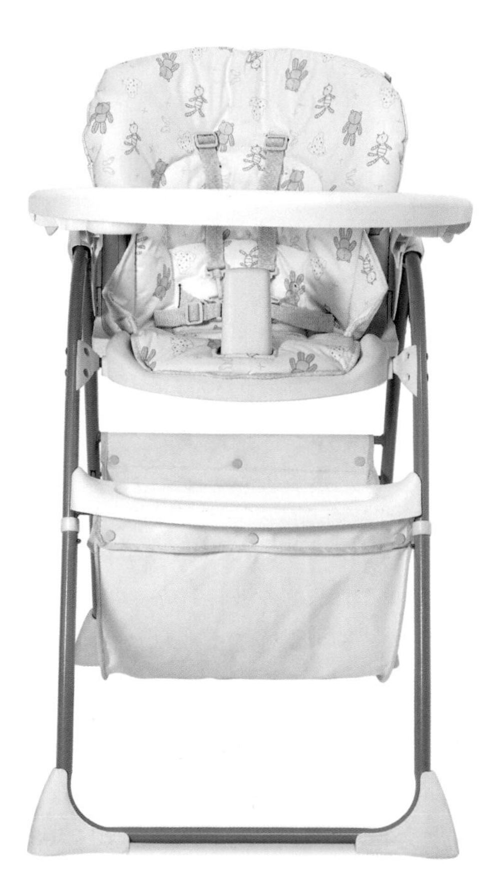

Bowls, plates and cups are best made of unbreakable materials. You don't actually need anything special – just see what's available and if it looks useful, buy it. Cups with lids, spouts and handles are the only ones very young babies can manage without help. The lidless 'Doidy' cup, made to slant so babies can manage to tip without spilling, has been around at least three generations, and some babies like it.

Ordinary teaspoons are fine, but small-bowled plastic baby ones may be useful. Hot washing of bowls, cups and spoons is all that's needed.

You will also need plenty of bibs. Plastic-backed ones prevent food and drinks leaking through to stain clothing.

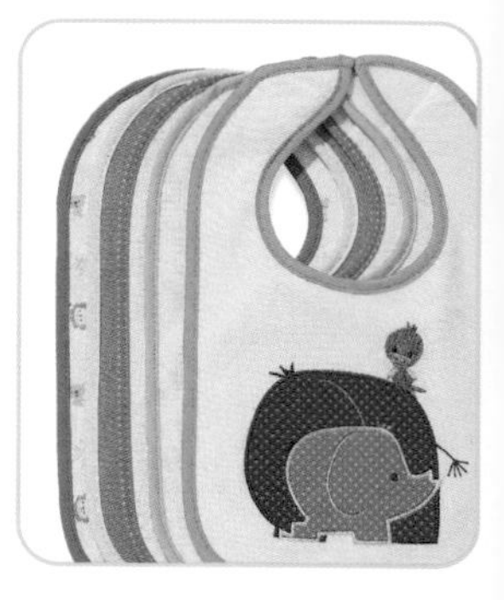

What does my baby need?

When your baby is building up her intake of solid foods, she will still get most of her calories and most of her nourishment from breast milk or formula. So worrying about how much food your baby has is usually not necessary – just serve up good-quality, fresh food of different types and textures and make eating enjoyable and varied.

After the age of six months, help your baby towards a healthy diet by avoiding processed, high-salt, high-sugar foods, and encouraging her to eat different types of fruit, vegetables, and foods which provide her with iron (good sources are dark green vegetables, meat, eggs and pulses). Continue to avoid whole nuts and honey (see box, above).

Very early weaning

If your baby has solids before the age of four months, these are the foods you should avoid:

- Wheat and foods containing wheat, as they contain the protein gluten (some authorities recommend gluten avoidance until six months as a way of reducing allergy).
- Nuts can cause allergy and are a choking hazard.
- Eggs (though the egg in bought baby foods is fine as it is pasteurised).
- Shellfish pose a risk of infection.
- Unpasteurised cheeses pose a risk of infection.
- Honey (tiny risk of botulism).

Even if you've chosen the purée and spoon route to weaning, let your baby practise self-feeding at least some of the time. Ideas for finger foods you can try include:

- Vegetable portions – babies enjoy holding broccoli or cauliflower by the stalks. Don't give uncooked vegetables, even if they can normally be eaten raw: carrot sticks, for example, could be a choking hazard.

WHAT SORT OF MILK?

Normal, full-fat, pasteurised milk is fine for your baby from the age of six months, in cooking or as an occasional drink. Don't use it as a main drink until the age of 12 months. While it is not harmful, large amounts could take the place of other foods, or indeed breast milk or formula, which your baby still needs. Don't give skimmed or semi-skimmed milk; they contain no fat-soluble vitamins, and are lower in calories than your baby needs.

If your baby is formula fed, you don't need to change to 'follow-on' formula. Follow-on is heavily marketed as being higher in iron than regular formula, but babies normally don't need the greater quantities.

Breastfed babies can still be fed responsively, as they readily adjust their intake to match their needs. Your baby may still feed often, but it seems the volume she takes will be lessened. If you want to reduce your baby's feeding frequency, or find this is inevitable as you have returned to work, then this is usually manageable as well. When your baby has a breastfeed, she probably will take a greater volume to make up for the fewer opportunities.

If your baby is bottlefed, she may need to be offered less – either smaller or fewer bottles, or use a cup. By the age of 12 months, a baby should be having around 500 ml of formula in addition to solids. Too much formula can take the place of the varied diet a growing baby needs. In addition, frequent bottlefeeding can affect dental health (see page 115). 'Nursing bottle caries' – tooth decay associated with the use of a bottle – happens when the teeth are bathed many times a day in milk (fruit drinks, squash or soft drinks are even worse). If your baby still wants to drink from a bottle more than occasionally, then put water in it.

WHICH BOUGHT BABY FOODS?

Prepared baby foods are subject to legislation, and artificial colours, flavours and other additives are not permitted. Salt and sugar levels are also kept low. Many cheaper baby foods contain thickeners which reduce their overall nutritive quality; more expensive brands may actually be better value for this reason. Read the labels – the 'best' baby foods have ingredients which are recognisable as items you could imagine using and eating yourself.

You can make your own fresh baby foods and purée or mash and then freeze in small amounts for later use; this is a lot easier than messing around with tiny amounts of peeled, chopped and cooked vegetables just for your baby. Or adapt family food, by removing your baby's portion before adding salt.

- Fruit slices or cubes, but avoid anything too hard – ripe pear is good.
- Chopped-up ham, chicken, pork (make sure there are no bones).
- Hard-boiled egg, chopped or sliced.
- Toast, bread, pitta bread, bread sticks.
- Crackers or oatcakes.

Finger foods are also good for between-meal snacks – babies and toddlers can't take large amounts of food at any one time, and most need a snack mid-morning and mid-afternoon.

Continue to breastfeed or formula feed. Introduce a cup by having one available at each meal time, and encouraging your baby to use it, with plain water or very diluted fruit juice. Avoid squash and drinks because their high sugar content is so bad for teeth and they contain artificial flavourings.

CHAPTER 9

Q&A: your questions answered

No book can cover every single special situation, but the questions here will deal with particular circumstances that haven't appeared in the other chapters.

Worldwide, breastfeeding specialists, lactation consultants and infant feeding experts have collectively come across many individual mothers and babies, and these days, conferences, journals, internet forums and mailing lists keep them in touch with one another. This community is very open to sharing its expertise, and if there is a question you need answering that's not here or elsewhere in the book, you can seek help from one of the sources on page 144; in turn, they have easy access to thousands of colleagues who may know.

Here, I have written questions based on the queries I've seen and heard, and in many cases, handled in my own experience as a breastfeeding counsellor. They're from the real world, where people don't always slot into chapters!

Q How will I know my baby is OK on breast milk and getting enough?

A In the first week, look for these signs that breastfeeding is going well:

- Your baby's stools change from black, sticky stuff (meconium) in the first couple of days, to brownish-green on day 2 to 3, to soft yellow on day 3 to 4 onwards. A baby who's feeding well will usually produce two to three soft yellow poos a day in the first weeks.
- Your baby's weight falls in the first few days, by up to about 10 per cent, reaching its lowest point on day 3 to 4, and then it starts rising (most babies regain all the weight they have lost by day 10 to14).
- Your baby is keen to feed, and feeds frequently, day and night – at least eight times, but double that is normal too.

If your baby isn't showing these signs, then feed him more often, using both breasts, and ask an experienced person to check he is transferring milk. Sometimes, babies just look as if they are feeding – they're happy enough at the breast and seem contented. But there's not a lot actually going in. A baby who sleeps a lot – three or four or more hours at a time, more than just very occasionally – may be conserving energy because he's not feeding well. So don't assume that a sleepy baby is a well-fed baby.

Q What about later on? Do I just judge all is well from my baby's weight?

A Weight is only one aspect of your baby's health, but it's a useful one to keep track of. A baby who has regained his

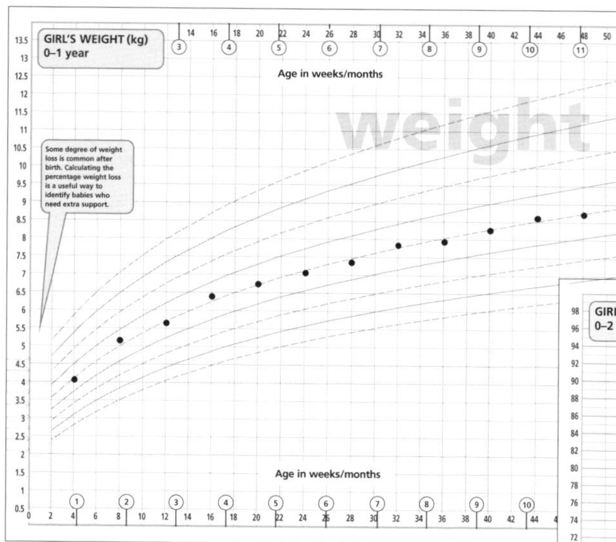

Boys and girls have different percentile charts because their growth rates and patterns differ. On these growth charts there are nine lines, which represent the 0.4th, 2nd, 9th, 25th, 50th, 75th, 91st, 98th and 99.6th percentiles. The 50th line represents the average for a particular age group.

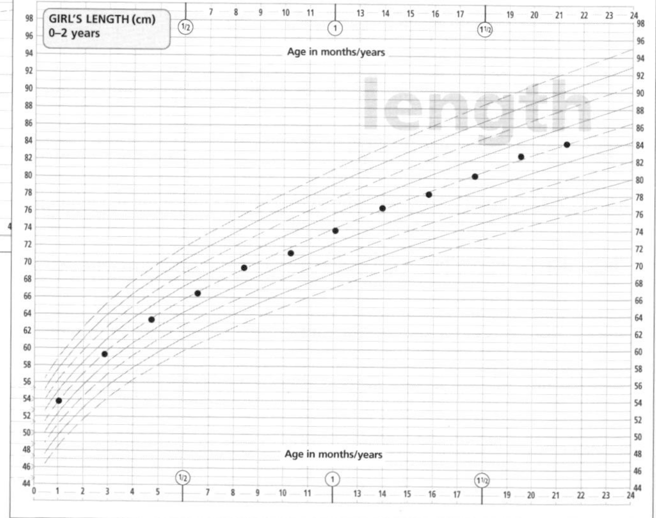

birthweight doesn't need weighing often – current guidance is to weigh healthy babies no more often than once a month up to six months, and no more than once every two months between then and a year.

Your baby's weight is plotted on a chart, and this helps give an overall picture of his progress in this area. Weight charts are pre-printed with curves, called percentiles, on a graph. The curves show that babies grow at a roughly predictable rate, remaining more or less on the same percentile as they do so. Out of 100 babies, a baby on the 50th percentile is lighter than 49 babies and heavier than the other 49 babies. A baby on the 25th percentile is heavier than 24 babies, and lighter than 74.

It can be normal for babies to go across one or two percentile spaces (the gaps between the percentiles on the chart), either upwards or downwards. If the health visitor or doctor sees more of a difference than this, then you'll probably be asked about how your baby's feeding, and whether there are any problems. If it looks like your baby would benefit from a closer look to see why the percentile is now that much higher or lower, then you will probably be referred to a dietitian or a paediatrician.

Growth spurts?

Q I've heard I have to watch out for 'growth spurts' – and that they mean frequent feeding. Is this right?

A Babies don't have a never-changing appetite, or a stable and predictable need for comfort and closeness. They grow at different rates, too. Some babies will go through a period of a few days when they indicate by their fussiness, hunger, and wakefulness that they need more attention from you and more chances to feed. This behaviour has been linked with growth spurts – the baby's physiological need to grow more at this particular time spurs him on to create more opportunities to feed. I have never seen convincing evidence that this is the reason behind these 'events', or anything that indicates they happen at predictable ages. The best thing is to

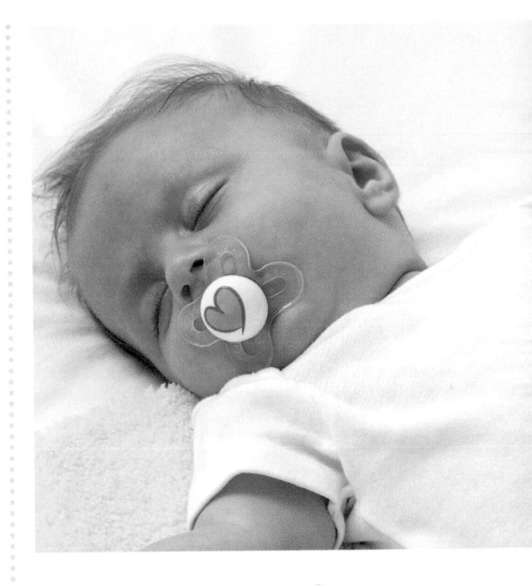

accept that many babies will have times when they show they need less sleep and more contact/more feeding ... and to roll with it!

Dummies?

Q Should I give my baby a dummy? He seems to like sucking a lot.

A Babies enjoy sucking – they have a powerful instinct to do so. Some research has suggested that if your baby uses a dummy, he should have it whenever he falls asleep for a long period: not having a dummy when a baby normally has one seems to increase the risk of SIDS on that particular occasion. There's no good evidence that deliberately introducing a dummy is protective in any way. Babies who are breastfed should only have dummies when breastfeeding is well-established and the baby is seen to be gaining weight normally; otherwise, it may be the baby satisfies his sucking on the dummy, not the breast, and this can interfere with building up a good milk supply.

Pregnancy and breastfeeding

Q I'm pregnant. Can I continue to breastfeed? And what happens when the baby comes if my first child has not stopped by then?

A Yes, you can continue. Some women find their breasts and nipples become a little sensitive in pregnancy, and their milk supply falls, though it does not usually disappear. When the baby comes you will produce colostrum. 'Tandem nursing' is the term given to breastfeeding a baby and a toddler at the same time. This might be literally true some of the time, and at other times you'll feed one at a time. It's unlikely you'll feed the toddler as often as you feed the baby, though.

Breastfeeding the next baby

Q My toddler will be aged just two when our baby is born. I would love to breastfeed this baby, but I didn't manage more than a couple of days first time around. How will my toddler react if she asks if she was breastfed as a baby and I have to say 'no'? And will she grow up thinking the baby got 'more' of me than she did?

A This is a common concern, all part of the worries mothers have about sharing themselves around more than one baby. Your toddler will just accept that this is how this baby gets milk, and that she got milk in a different way. She won't think of it as getting less of you – her own experience of your love, attention, involvement and care is what counts, not whether she knows if she was breastfed or not. If the

conversation ever comes up when she is older, you can just explain that breastfeeding was something you found difficult the first time, and you used formula to make sure she didn't go hungry.

Jealous toddler

Q **My memory of breastfeeding my first baby is that it took a long time, and that I didn't have time for much else. How am I going to manage to breastfeed my next baby, and have the time to give to my toddler as well, and will my toddler be jealous when he sees me feeding all the time?**

A One good thing about breastfeeding is that it gives you a spare arm and hand to read a book with your toddler, build a brick tower, play a game, share a hug. This is not so easy when you're bottlefeeding. Breastfeeding can take up more 'sofa time' at first, but there's no time taken up preparing bottles, washing and sterilising. Caring for two children is a juggling act, however you feed. There's no evidence that toddlers are more jealous, or more likely to be jealous, if their siblings are breastfed. Try to make sure your toddler has you to himself for a guaranteed period every day – just 10 minutes when there are just the two of you while the baby sleeps helps a lot.

Refusal to breastfeed

Q **My baby was a keen breastfeeder and in the past day he's just refused to do more than take a few sucks. He's eight months. What could be upsetting him about breastfeeding?**

A A young baby – up to a few months old – who refuses to feed needs checking out by your health visitor or doctor. What you read next only applies to older babies who appear to be well.

A refusal to feed is known as 'nursing strike' and it can happen for lots of reasons, and you may just have to guess at which might apply:

- teething making feeding irritating or sore;
- your baby is upset and confused because of a different environment, a busy day, a new carer, being separated from you;
- he had a fright when feeding (perhaps a very loud noise disturbed him and made him cry);
- you are about to start a period (this can make the milk taste different).

Almost always, gentle patience and encouragement mean a baby 'on strike' returns to the breast after a short while. Babies like this sometimes feed well at night, or when sleepy, so choose these moments to offer. Try feeding in a different position – even standing up if you can. This sometimes breaks the 'spell'.

Good side, bad side?

Q **Is it possible for a baby to have a favourite breast and to reject the other one?**

A Yes – sometimes you can overcome the resistance to the 'lesser' one by moving him towards it across your body, so he doesn't realise he's switched (or accepts the switch, because his body is facing the same way). Keep on offering for a while, though if your baby really doesn't budge in his rejection, it's perfectly possible to feed from one side only all the time. You can gently hand express the other to relieve any uncomfortable fullness if you need to. Over a period of a few weeks, production on the 'unused' breast will cease. You will have sufficient milk in the 'remainder' – and any lopsideness will diminish over the same time.

Refuses a bottle – help!

Q I've decided my baby will need some bottles when I go back to work – I might express if I can, or else she will need formula. She will be five months old when this happens, and she is four months now. Problem is she hates the bottle and pushes it away. She now screams when she sees it. How will I be sure she can manage when I am not there to breastfeed?

A There are different ways to encourage a reluctant bottlefeeder and after a week or so 'off' to help your baby forget she doesn't like bottles and teats, you can work your way through this:

- have someone else give the bottle (you should be out of the room);
- let her have the bottle to play with, and use it as a toy yourself (hiding it, making it pop up again, tickling her cheeks with it);
- offer her the bottle as close and skin-to-skin as you would with a breastfeed ...
- ... or conversely, feed her with it face-to-face, with her in her chair;
- try a cup with a teat, rather than a bottle, so it looks different;
- try when she is sleepy and very relaxed;
- try a different teat with a different feel in her mouth (for example, latex if you have been using silicone, or vice versa) or one with a different shape.

A baby of four months old or more can be helped to take a drink from a cup, if she is adamant bottles just won't do.

Nipples right for my baby?

Q How do I know if my nipples will be OK for my baby? Mine seem a bit flat, though I have been told that they change a bit in pregnancy.

A Yes, nipples do change in pregnancy, and they may become more prominent. But nipple and breasts come in all shapes and sizes, and there's no reason to assume your baby won't manage just fine. Maybe you will need a little more help at first to assist your baby to get latched on, if your nipples are very flat. If your nipples are inverted – like a dimple at the very end – you may find your baby is adept at drawing them out. You can buy a gadget called a 'nipple everter' quite cheaply over the internet or from a pharmacy and some women who have experienced difficulty with inverted nipples have found it useful.

Breast issues

Q My breasts have suddenly gone soft and they feel empty. Have I stopped making milk all of a sudden, with my baby just 12 weeks old? He only stays on the breast a few minutes now – is this because there's not much milk?

A No – this change is normal, though it's not always sudden. What happens is that your breasts have less fat in them now, and they have milk-producing tissue in them instead. In addition, you are probably not 'over producing' milk any more, and your supply is matching your baby's needs more closely. The net result is that your breasts feel empty, but they're not. Short feeds are normal, too, for an older baby.

No milk?

Q My mother tells me she had no milk when her babies were born. I'm worried the same thing will happen to me.

A Literally no milk is very rare. There are some physical conditions that make it hard to build a good supply. Sheehan's syndrome (caused by a major postnatal bleed that affects the pituitary gland); retained placenta; a pituitary tumour; thyroid problems; and severe anaemia are all conditions which can have an impact on milk production. They are all treatable. A very few women don't have sufficient breast-milk-making tissue and they may struggle, too – their breasts appear 'tubular' in shape. None of these conditions is hereditary.

Leaky breasts

Q Do all mothers leak between breastfeeds?

A Some do – it varies. If you leak, you can wear breastpads inside your bra which absorb the milk. It can be especially troublesome at night, so you might need extra protection – large, folded up handkerchiefs help, or some other absorbent fabric you can wash and use again. It's normally something that settles down after the first couple of months or so.

Breastfeeding and implants?

Q Can I breastfeed with implants, or should I have them removed before I get pregnant?

A Yes, you can breastfeed. Plenty of women have done this. There is no evidence of the milk, or the baby, being affected in any way, so no need for removal.

Surgery and breastfeeding

Q What about breastfeeding after surgery to reduce breast size or for any other reason? Does this mean breastfeeding can't happen?

A Sometimes surgery severs the ducts, or re-sites the nipple, and this means breastfeeding might be more difficult – but don't assume that it will be impossible. There are information resources to help (see page 144).

Breastfeeding and adoption

Q Is it possible to breastfeed without even being pregnant? I have heard adoptive mothers can do it.

A Yes, it is. It's easier if you have breastfed before, but there are many cases of women who have adopted babies, or who have become mothers of surrogate babies (where another woman had the pregnancy and birth), and who have succeeded in producing breast milk. You need to prepare with a breast pump, and be willing to use it – a lot! This produces 'induced lactation'. The baby can come to the breast and be supplemented with formula at the breast by means of a 'nursing supplementer' which delivers formula down a tube taped to the nipple. So the baby gets what breast milk there is, alongside the formula which keeps up the 'reward' for continuing to suckle. Working up to producing a full supply for an adopted/surrogate baby seems to be very unusual, but managing at least some, if not most, of the baby's breast milk needs is certainly achievable. Mothers who have done this report that the effort and the rewards that come from the effort become an important part of their relationship with their babies.

Formula guilt

Q I've been told I should never have given my breastfed baby formula when he was newborn, and that I have destroyed his 'virgin gut'. Apparently there's no way I should even bother to breastfeed now because I have undone all the good I might have done. Is this true?

A The 'virgin gut' is a description of the baby's metabolism when it is 'untouched' by any formula. The theory behind it comes from the observation that anything other than breast milk changes the 'environment' of the gut, by affecting the type of intestinal flora (bacterial micro-organisms sometimes called 'good bacteria') it produces. This is thought to increase the baby's risk of allergy and disease. However, this does not mean there is permanent or even long-lasting damage to the gut. The exceptions to this are cases where there may be severe allergy, or if the baby is at risk of maternal-to-infant transmission of HIV, where solely breastfeeding, or solely formula feeding – and not mixed feeding – are the safest feeding methods.

A breastfed baby who has had some formula benefits from continued breastfeeding and can return to full breastfeeding.

My feeling is that the phrase is unnecessarily purist and somewhat undermining to mothers. Sometimes, the virgin gut theory is quoted in a way that makes mothers who have given, or who continue to give, formula feel criticised and a bit helpless – after all, you can't turn back the clock and 'ungive' your baby formula. In your case, you can continue breastfeeding happily and confident that your baby is being well-fed and enjoying the protection breastfeeding gives him.

Regrets?

Q When I look back at the time I breastfed my baby, I still have regrets I did not do it for longer. I tried very hard, and I felt people were sometimes pressurising me to stop, and sometimes pressurising me to continue. I was very mixed up and I wanted just

to feed without having a great performance each time, and without the worry afterwards about whether he had had enough, or was going to cry. This was so stressful, I felt relieved in some ways when I switched to formula. Once I could share the feeding, and it was not all down to me, I could relax. My baby no longer had a stressed-out mum, and I could just enjoy him. The trouble is, I still think I could have done a bit more ... and I get so cross and upset when I hear people bang on about how wonderful breastfeeding is: it wasn't wonderful for me! Is there a way of reframing your memories?

A Any breastfeeding is helpful to your baby's health – even just one day, and even just one feed, gives your baby a 'dose' of antibodies against infection. The more you breastfed, the more protection your baby got from you. You can also start thinking of feeding as more than just health. Of course it's a factor, and it matters how babies are fed, but it is not the only thing that matters. As you found, being unstressed and better able to relate and respond to your baby has huge benefits, too.

Talking to other mothers about your feelings will show you are not alone. Some mothers who formula feed do feel judged and criticised, and are very sensitive to any idea that their way of feeding has something to do with their worth as mothers. These feelings should lessen in time, and if they don't, if they get stronger or you feel as upset about what went on as you did in the first weeks after you switched, then speak to your health visitor. Counselling or another form of talking therapy might help you a lot.

Nothing in life is as simple as 'breast or bottle?', and the 'choice' to go for one or the other, or a combination, is dependent on many factors, some of them personal to the individual mother herself ... as you found!

Index and acknowledgements

Suppliers

Thanks to the following companies for supplying products/photography: Babybjorn p123. Mothercare, for equipment shown p128.

Illustrations

Amanda Williams p51.

Photolibrary.com

Jacket, pp 2, 4, 5, 6, 7, 12, 14, 24, 25, 26, 30, 33, 35, 38, 39, 40, 42, 44, 46, 52, 53, 60, 63, 64, 65, 71, 72, 74, 78, 84, 90, 95, 96, 103, 107, 112, 116, 118, 124, 126, 127, 129, 130, 141.

Science Photo Library

p75 AJ Photo/Science Photo Library, p77 Science Photo Library.

Getty Images

pp 85, 105, 136, 139.

Author's acknowledgements

Thanks to the many thousands of parents I have encountered over the past 30 years of supporting breastfeeding; the many hundreds of colleagues I have got to know by email over the past 15 years; the many scores of women I have trained and supported in this work; the many dozens of friends I have worked with in NCT. I owe a lot to NCT, but the words in this book are mine, and any errors, opinions or oddities are mine, too, not NCT's.
www.heatherwelford.co.uk

Further information

Information on women's feelings about using formula (page 102) can be read in 'Mothers' experiences of, and attitudes to, using infant formula in the early months' by Dr Ellie Lee and Professor Frank Furedi. You can find this report on the web.

Professor Helen Ball's research on parents, babies and bed sharing has a home on the web at www.dur.ac.uk/sleep.lab/

For information on breastfeeding beyond babyhood, read *Breastfeeding Older Children* by Ann Sinnott (Free Association Books, 2009). The author shares the experience of many women and children, and explores the social and cultural aspects of this choice.

To find out more about weaning by letting your baby feed himself, read *Baby-led Weaning: Helping Your Baby to Love Good Food* by Gill Rapley and Tracey Murkett (Vermillion, 2008).

For more about the way babies develop as a response to the way they are cared for, read *What Every Parent Needs to Know: The incredible effects of love, nurture and play on your child's development* by Margot Sunderland (Dorling Kindersley, 2007).

The UNICEF Baby Friendly Initiative is a worldwide programme, which aims to improve hospital and healthcare professional practice, in order to protect breastfeeding. You can read the details at www.babyfriendly.org

Baby Milk Action protects breastfeeding and protects babies fed on formula. They can be found at www.info.babymilkaction.org/

Help with breastfeeding

You may live near a breastfeeding support group, and/or have supportive and knowledgeable help from healthcare professionals. Some areas have trained peer supporters who are able to share basic information with you and to offer friendship and support for breastfeeding. Or you can speak to a breastfeeding counsellor, normally trained to a high level and available at support groups or in person, after initial phone contact.
In the UK, the following volunteer helplines can put you in touch with one:
National Breastfeeding Helpline
0300 100 0212
National Childbirth Trust
0300 330 0771
Breastfeeding Network
0300 100 0210
La Leche League
0845 1202918
Association of Breastfeeding Mothers
08444 122949

Some breastfeeding counsellors may also help with non-medical questions about formula feeding. If you are using formula, or have used formula, don't think you are somehow excluded from talking to a breastfeeding counsellor. We are used to speaking to mothers in all sorts of feeding circumstances, and we don't judge, criticise or tell you what to do.

In some countries, you can find help with breastfeeding from an IBCLC (international board certified lactation consultant). This is an international qualification.